Praise for Richard Abanes's
Incisive Research and Analysis of Today's Culture

THE TRUTH BEHIND THE DA VINCI CODE

"A well-written and thorough examination...Everyone confused by Dan Brown's novel should read this book."

—TIM LAHAYE, megaselling coauthor
of the Left Behind® series

"Highly readable...well-organized and accessible."

—FAITHFULREADER.COM

RICK WARREN AND THE PURPOSE THAT DRIVES HIM

"Thank you, Richard Abanes, for setting the record straight."

—LEE STROBEL, journalist and bestselling
author of *The Case for a Creator*

"A balanced, fair analysis that separates fact from fiction regarding Warren's ministry and teachings."

—DR. RON RHODES, bestselling
author of *Angels Among Us*

HARRY POTTER, NARNIA, AND THE LORD OF THE RINGS

"Should be on the shelf of every educator, youth worker, and parent interested in our culture's fascination with fantasy...An honest, straightforward, and vitally important tool."

—BILL MYERS, bestselling youth and
children's fiction author

"Fascinating and thoroughly enjoyable, yet grounded in scholarship of the highest quality. This book should be in every home."

—MICHAEL O'BRIEN, bestselling author
of the Father Elijah series

WHAT EVERY PARENT
NEEDS TO KNOW ABOUT
VIDEO
GAMES

RICHARD ABANES

HARVEST HOUSE PUBLISHERS

EUGENE, OREGON

Cover by Terry Dugan Design, Minneapolis, Minnesota

Cover photos © Jupiterimages; Colin Anderson / Brand X Pictures / Alamy

WHAT EVERY PARENT NEEDS TO KNOW ABOUT VIDEO GAMES
Copyright © 2006 by Richard Abanes
Published by Harvest House Publishers
Eugene, Oregon 97402
www.harvesthousepublishers.com

Library of Congress Cataloging-in-Publication Data
Abanes, Richard.
    What every parent needs to know about video games / Richard Abanes.
        p. cm.
    ISBN-13: 978-0-7369-1740-7
    ISBN-10: 0-7369-1740-3
    1. Video games—Handbooks, manuals, etc. 2. Video games—Moral and ethical aspects.
    3. Video games and children. I. Title.
    GV1469.3.A23 2006
    794.8—dc22   2006001451

Printed in the United States of America

06 07 08 09 10 11 12 13 14 / LB-MS / 10 9 8 7 6 5 4 3 2 1

Contents

This book discusses video and computer games that contain depictions of violence and sex. Some material—including certain photos of game content—may be unsuitable for children and teens. Parental discretion is advised.

The Next Generation

The thing about video games that makes them
so special is that we're given free rein to explore worlds,
to interact with magnificent creatures of fantasy, to travel
through spaces that could only live in the imagination.

BRADY FIECHTER
executive editor, *Play*

Hollywood, radio, and even MTV are all being pushed aside. Into their slot are moving video games, perhaps the most influential pop-culture force in recent memory. At your fingertips—literally—there now reside a host of other worlds, different dimensions of time, and alternate realities to explore. And their number continues to increase at a staggeringly rapid rate. Steve Schnur, worldwide music executive for EA Games, has suggested that video games "are what MTV used to be: being hip, being current, ushering in trends, and single-handedly created 'cool.'"[1]

You've Come a Long Way, Baby

Video games can no longer be thought of as little more than meaningless distractions designed to fill the playtime of children. According to Benjamin Porcari—founder and president of IBC

Digital (the company in charge of creating content for MTV2's *Video Mods* program)— "More sophisticated games and exciting content have pushed games out into the mainstream of entertainment."[2]

Porcari is not exaggerating. According to the most recent sales figures, the "overall worth of the video game industry worldwide is projected to grow from $25 billion in 2004 to $55 billion in 2009." Some observers have suggested, with good reason, that "games currently represent, financially, the highest-growth area in the entertainment business." This holds especially true of adult male consumers who "prefer paying for video games over any form of music….Games are now second only to DVDs for men as a purchase category."[3]

Signs of the growing prosperity and influence of the video-game industry are everywhere. For example, expos and competitions are now common (see sidebar)—as are video-game sporting events. Yes, I said sporting events. Playing video games has become so competitive that it has achieved legitimate sport status on an international level (complete with large monetary prizes). These "e-sports" might easily turn into Olympic events in the not-too-distant future…with USA Rebels battling Korean Imperial Guards for the gold, but doing so on a distant fantasy world.

Video games have even crossed over into television, as evidenced by the MTV2 program *Video Mods*, which uses characters from popular video games to "create brand new music videos for today's hits" by well-known bands, such as Evanescence.[6] (One such pairing resulted in a new music video version of Franz Ferdinand's "Take Me Out" that featured Jedi masters Obi-Wan Kenobi and Yoda—from the *Star Wars: Episode III* game—

playing guitar and drums, respectively, and Anakin Skywalker singing lead vocals.)

Conventions, Expos, Competitions

The MTV2/Nesquick-sponsored Game Riot conference in 2005 included a video-game party, competition between amateurs, and for those brave enough, an opportunity to match skills with professional video-game player Matt Leto (a.k.a. Zyos), the undisputed reigning *Halo* champ.[4]

Consider, too, the annual GenCon in Indianapolis, which attracts some 50,000 international gaming enthusiasts, who show up at the city's convention center to celebrate "just about every type of gaming and game-related activity you can imagine."[5]

And then there is the annual Electronic Entertainment Expo (E^3)—the big kahuna of all such gatherings. (Finally, I must mention the October 2005 IGN Live convention and also BlizzCon—a conference dedicated to the wildly popular online game *World of Warcraft*. I had a spectacular time at both of these events.)

And That's Not All

Like the 1980s Toyota commercials exclaimed, "Who could ask for anything more?" Well, the surprising answer is, a lot of people. The year 2005, for instance, saw the emergence of a concert tour that presented music from video games as performed by "top orchestras and choirs combined with video footage, lasers, lights, and live action to create an explosive and unique entertainment experience." This concert treated video game fans to the lush musical scores from top-selling video games such as *Halo, Final Fantasy, Advent Rising,* and *Castlevania.* Another concert tour featured music taken exclusively from *Final Fantasy,* performed by "prestigious local orchestras and choirs."[7]

Given the innovation and creativity that now surround video games, it is no surprise that 2005 also saw "the world's first cable channel devoted entirely to video games" being launched. Not to be outdone, the Turner Broadcasting System has created GameTap (www.gametap.com)—a broadband entertainment network featuring "a wealth of classic and current console, arcade, and PC" video-game titles for $14.95 a month.[8] This network has been set up for subscribers interested in accessing hundreds, eventually thousands, of family-friendly games (as opposed to "Mature"-rated games).

Countless bands and musicians are jumping on the video-game bandwagon as well. In the very near future there will undoubtedly be CD album soundtracks to video games just like there are now CD album soundtracks to films and theatrical productions. Tim Riley, music supervisor at Activision, notes that for up-and-coming artists, "getting a spot on a soundtrack can be as powerful as being added to a radio station's playlist."[9]

But here's the real pop-culture kicker—there are now even a number of Christian video games being created, such as *Armageddon* (a "shooter" game—see page 30) and *Left Behind: Eternal Forces,* a "real-time strategy game based on the bestselling books by Tim LaHaye and Jerry Jenkins." According to Garland Wong, president of the company working on *Armageddon,* "There's a huge potential for Christian content" in video games—even mature/violent games that include war, bloodshed, and frightening images. As Wong says, "We're trying to approach it from a realistic perspective."[10]

Troy Lyndon of Left Behind Games agrees that a realistic, contemporary, and provocative approach is the way to go:

> The only way Christian gaming will appeal to the mass market will be if we make quality games and create games with stimulating points that allow the gamers to think for themselves without insulting their intelligence or attempting to outright convert them.[11]

Clearly, video games have become big business. So big, in fact, that several corporations are now using in-game product placement to sell their wares. In 2003 this tactic ("advergaming") garnered $79 million in revenue. By 2008 "these practices may generate $206 million or more."[12] But the success has not come without controversy.

The Fly in the Warp Drive

Image-based video games (as opposed to text-based games) were controversial almost as soon as they hit the entertainment scene in the 1980s. What were these "games"? Why were kids so attracted to them? How might they benefit—or harm—children? Some forward-thinking observers of pop culture expressed excitement, while others were less than kind. The renowned child behaviorist Dr. Benjamin Spock, for instance, snubbed video games by labeling them as nothing but a "colossal waste of time."[13]

But Dr. Spock's swipe at video games is nothing compared to what is happening today. The Chinese government, for example, has adopted tough video-game restrictions in recent years. At one point, it even attempted to control how much time Chinese citizens devoted to playing. This has all been in an effort to, as they indicate, "create a healthier environment for children, lumping games in with the more obvious vices of gambling and porn."[14]

In the United States, too, some laws have been enacted to control the distribution of video games to minors. The reasoning in China bears a striking similarity to the reasoning in America. Consider the words of California Assemblyman Leland Yee (a Democrat from San Francisco), whose efforts to control video-game distribution led to the passage of a new law in his state that prohibits the sale of certain games to minors (see chapter 2):

> As a child psychologist, I understand the harmful effects these games have on our children....Study after study of the most respected medical organizations has shown that these ultra-violent video games have negative effects on our kids....[It has been shown that] children who play these ultra-violent video games are more likely to view violence as an effective way of settling conflicts; that these games can lead to emotional desensitization toward violence in real life; and that such children have a higher tendency for violent and aggressive behavior later in life.[15]

Yee's arguments sound convincing, especially in light of some horrific crimes that investigators have loosely linked to video-game playing. For example, the Columbine High School killers (Eric Harris and Dylan Klebold) enjoyed playing *Doom*, a "first-person shooter" game. And in Alabama a 20-year-old man "obsessed with the *Grand Theft Auto* game" (a game infamous for its violence) shot and killed two policemen and a police dispatcher.[16] But did *Grand Theft Auto* really desensitize this man to murder and prompt his attacks? Did *Doom* actually train Harris and Klebold to kill fellow students?

Anti-video-game protestors, legislators, and parents would answer with a strong yes to both questions. Gamers, on the other hand, would say, "Certainly not!" Both camps, of course, are adamant. So adamant, in fact, that a kind of mini culture war has erupted, with nongamers pitted against gamers—and the sides are divided strikingly along generational lines, which is significant.

Although a full 50 percent of Americans play video games, most of today's gamers (around 75 percent) are under 40 years old. In other words, they are the generation raised on games. This translates into a new kind of generation gap between older nongamers and young-adult gamers (as well as teens and children). Conflict and controversy has resulted.

But things are changing, especially as young gamers grow older and begin to slowly take the reins of social and cultural power and gain more influence in the media. So far, though, it has not been an easy transition. John Davison, editorial director for Ziff Davis's Game Group, has rightly observed, "Like comic books and hip-hop music before them, video games are currently fueling a firestorm of media controversy."[17]

And Davison is not alone in taking this view. His insightful article "Pop Culture Pariah" cites Patricia Vance—president of the Entertainment Software Ratings Board (ESRB)—as another industry personality who "believes the mainstream media is cherry-picking facts about gaming to show the industry in a bad light. 'Few games are M-rated [for Mature content],' she points out, 'but that's the type of game the mainstream media always shows when they want to drive home any point about video games.'"[18]

A Personal Take

For me, a week begins in a faraway galaxy where I am a member of the Gallente Federation. I pilot a variety of spaceships including a swift little frigate, a cargo hauler, a menacing destroyer known as a Thrasher, several high-level cruisers, and a battleship. My primary vessel takes me on a variety of missions during which I am invariably forced to combat smugglers, spies from rival federations (or factions), and all sorts of other nasties that inhabit the solar system that I call home (Angel Cartel space pirates, for example, immediately come to mind).

By Thursday or Friday, however, I am usually back on Earth as a medic, either in the midst of a World War II campaign or in the thick of a modern military conflict (usually around the Middle East). While in these situations I am a dedicated soldier whose heart and mind are intently focused on saving as many lives as possible in spite of sniper attacks, airstrikes, and barrages of heavy artillery.

Then comes the weekend, which invariably finds me stuck in a place known only as "City #17." I am a man confused, dazed, worried...and running for his life. I have no idea exactly how I got to City #17, nor do I understand very much about what is happening around me. But what I do know is that very little of it is good. My adventure leads me day after day on a path of discovery. What happened to me? Why am I here?

Where am I supposed to go next? How am I to survive another 24 hours? Through it all I am a man being hunted for some as yet undiscovered reason.

There are many more options available to me than these few characters I have briefly described. I'm not the best video-game player—not by any means. I fall somewhere in the middle of the pack with millions of other gamers who, like me, just love to play. We are part of a growing segment of society and culture that sees video games as a hobby, a sport, a route to relaxation, and even a livelihood (for example, gaming journalists and game story writers).

As one gamer eloquently expressed it, video games "are a great escape from a bland reality, a way to stimulate your mind and relax your soul in colorful, distant worlds that the talented minds of the creators have conceived."[19]

Here Comes the Future

There is no doubt that the influence and appeal of the electronic gaming industry will only grow as video and computer games are seen more and more as important forms of art and entertainment. The sheer money factor is enough to ensure the future of electronic games. But there are now other important aspects to video games.

For example, a new entertainment genre called *machinima* (from the words "machine cinema" or "machine animation") has emerged. It consists of taking recorded video footage from a game and adding original dialogue to the player-controlled movements of the characters. The new art form has became so popular so

Several of the ships I fly each day as a space pilot in Eve Online, which is one of the premier (perhaps even the best) massively multiplayer online role-playing games in existence (abbreviated as MMORPG).

Here we see my industrial ship (top left), which I use to haul trade goods and ore throughout the Eve universe. My battleship—known as a Megathron—is used for major combat missions, as in the above mission wherein I succeeded in destroying not only a slew of space pirates, but also an enemy outpost (top right). A smaller frigate-level ship I fly, called a Tristan, can also be used for combat. In this photo (below left) I have just obliterated an enemy structure.

Not all missions, however, are successful. On my first attempt to complete the "Silence the Informant" mission, my cruiser barely made it back to home port—hardly any shields remaining, no armor left, and hull almost gone. My ship, in fact, was on fire (below right). The various icons on the side of the screen are all of my ship controls and reference instruments.

Eve is one of the most visually appealing video games to date and also is family-friendly. (Screen shots courtesy of CCP, taken by Richard Abanes during game play.)

quickly that influential game industry movers and shakers have not only formed the Academy of Machinima Art and Science, but also have launched a yearly machinima film festival (in New York).

A new kind of photography/art is now emerging as well—screen shots* of in-game scenes (for example, landscapes, battles, character interaction) that a player can actually orchestrate via playing: "There is light and shadow, lines, curves, patterns, balance, close-ups, architecture, nature and many other elements of photography....Players can actually have a chance to 'compose' photos and even capture moments of emotion, decay, ruin, humanity, etc."[20]

As for actual game play, we will soon be able to play with on-screen characters that have very "realistic emotions." One near-future reality, for instance, might be a *Finding Nemo* video game that could "look just like the movie."[21] This means hyperrealistic scenery; movie-quality action; and characters that will not only look truly alive, but will also behave in ways that mirror the unpredictability of humans—via highly advanced artificial intelligence (AI).

And in a push toward making *Star Trek*'s "holodeck" a reality, a Finnish company has produced a life-sized room wherein a player's fight moves are interpreted by cameras and transferred on screen to their virtual reality characters, through whom players can battle an assortment of foes using various weapons.[22] Sony has even patented a new technology "that would beam sensory info

---

* A screen shot is "an image taken by the computer to record the visible items on the monitor or another visual output device." (Definition from www.Wikipedia.com.)

such as smells, tastes, and images straight to the brain," which could forever change the video-game playing experience.[23]

All of this is happening as the generation that grew up on video games is assuming its rightful place in the world. But with the emergence of today's young adults, some important questions about video games are beginning to surface. What makes a "good" video game? Does there exist any way of determining if the degree of aggression in a game is too much aggression? How should right and wrong be portrayed in a game? Where is the line between valid artistic expression through video games and an irresponsible abuse of America's freedoms of speech? Do video-game developers and publishers have any social, moral, or cultural responsibilities at all? Do video games actually affect the children, teens, and adults who play them? If so, how?

These are just some of the issues I explore in the following pages. My intention is for this volume to be a small, yet significant, contribution to what promises to someday be a vast collection of video-game-related literature. Clearly, the era of video games has arrived—and all of us are already a part of it.

1
Coming to Terms—
From RPG to FPS

Our art form [electronic games] is the only one
in which the person experiencing the entertainment
determines the outcome. You're not passively watching,
or reading, or listening, you are controlling, adventuring,
and achieving. We are something new.

—Jamil Moledina
director, Game Developers Conference

Despite their growing popularity, video games are only now beginning to garner the level of news coverage and respectability enjoyed by other arts and entertainment forms. Few people outside the gaming community know about the widely varying kinds of games available, their content, or what separates more family-friendly games from those that should clearly be played only by mature gamers (see ratings definitions in chapter 2).

Even journalists, taken as a whole, are lacking in knowledge about games. According to Seth Shiesel, video-game reporter for the *New York Times*, "A lot of people running media outlets now are of a different generation" than the video-game generation. "They didn't grow up playing games, and the notion of doing so is alien to them."[1] The first thing, therefore, that must be included in any guide is a clear and concise explanation of what kinds of games are available.

Role-Playing Games

A *role-playing game*, also known as simply an *RPG*, is one of the grandest and most beloved of all styles. Its origins can be traced directly to the *Dungeons and Dragons* board game, and then even further back to J.R.R. Tolkien's trilogy of books, The Lord of the Rings, which gave rise to *Dungeons and Dragons*.

The standard RPG involves the player assuming a character (for example, an elf, dwarf, warrior, or healer) and going on a series of journeys (that is to say, quests) by which the character advances in skill level, overall strength, and experience. These quests can either be individual or done in company with fellow travelers, all of whom are themselves trying to advance in skill, strength, and experience.

An RPG usually takes place in a mythical world, the distant past, or perhaps the distant future (or maybe even another dimension of reality altogether). Games in this genre include such popular titles as *Fable: The Lost Chapters; The Elder Scrolls IV: Oblivion;* and *Final Fantasy.* These games, like most RPGs, are very broad in scope, with a grand storyline that leads the player onward and upward (hopefully), ever increasing in prowess at being whatever kind of character they have chosen.

The Elder Scrolls IV: Oblivion, for instance, takes place in the world of Tamriel. The emperor in this tale has been assassinated and, as a player, it is your job to locate "a long-lost heir to the throne. Meanwhile, the gates of Oblivion (a sort of hell dimension in Tamriel) remain open, paving the way for a massive demon invasion."[2]

The RPG *Fable: The Lost Chapters* unfolds in "Albion," where you are a hero in training. Your task is to do nothing less than save the entire realm from mysterious evildoers called the "summoners." These horrifying creatures are stalking the land for an as yet unknown reason. To discover why they have appeared you must travel far and wide to places such as Lost Bay and the Desolate Northern Wastes.

Fable is an intricately crafted world wherein you can interact freely with all kinds of NPCs (*nonplaying characters*, which are computer-generated characters not being controlled by real people) in order to accomplish a multitude of challenging tasks. One aspect of *Fable* that makes it particularly elegant is how your moral choices affect not only the environment's appearance, but also the NPCs' responses to you. Such choices even affect your appearance! If you do bad and evil things, you start looking bad and evil. If you do good things, you appear righteous and honorable.

The typically vast size and scope of the RPG world is extremely attractive to players. There are usually an almost countless number of regions, cities, and structures that can be explored. This can lead to well over a hundred hours of game play just to discover everything! Add to that the ability to create more than one character and make different choices with that character during play, and you end up with a game that can give months, if not years, of entertainment—all for about $50.

(Other successful RPGs are *Baldur's Gate, Everquest, Icewind Dale, Neverwinter Nights, Guild Wars,* and *Dungeon Siege.*)

Massively Multiplayer Online Role-Playing Games

The genre of *massively multiplayer online role-playing games* is rather new and is a direct result of the Internet's presence in all parts of the globe. *MMORPGs* (or simply *MMOs*) are very much like regular RPGs in that they present the player with a character to "level up" in experiences, skills, knowledge, wisdom, and power(s). There are a few big differences, however, between regular RPGs and MMORPGs.

First, a player must not only buy the software needed to play the MMO (usually), but also pay a monthly subscription fee in order to play. Consequently, an MMO is really only good for someone who plans to spend many hours at play.

Second, all MMO players are *together* online. This is a marvelous way to make friendships with people halfway around the world. Everyone is connected inside the game and can communicate with each other.

The third and most important difference between MMOs and regular RPGs is this: Players can actually affect the world in which they play.

A Worldwide Platform

I play *Eve Online* (a science fiction MMO) for hours every week from my home in Southern California. But I regularly talk to people as far away as Iceland, Belgium, France, Sweden, and England. The game's reach is phenomenal. It is difficult to describe how stimulating such interaction can be, especially when everyone involved is speeding through space en route to various locations in the Eve universe. The real-time live chat channel is always abuzz with hundreds of players from all over the world.

"Hey! Is anyone in the region Sing Laison?" someone might ask.

Another pilot usually replies. "Yeah. Sing Laison here."

"Can you do me a favor and check the pricing of a '10MN Afterburner II' in that region?"

"Sure, selling over here for about 1.6 million ISK [Interstellar Standard Kredits]."

You can even decide on a destination in some solar system at which to meet each other in ships (for example, Moon 5, the Ommare solar system, in the Essence space region). After arriving at the location, you can fly anywhere you wish and do whatever you want to do.

And not all of the chatter, of course, is about in-game matters. People talk about all kinds of things: family, life, jobs, experiences, world politics, global tragedies, and personal accomplishments.

Being able to affect a game's environment is one of the most significant breakthroughs in the realm of video-gaming. MMO players can form guilds, teams, corporations, and other organized groups in hopes of causing change in the fantasy realm. As a player, you can buy, sell, or trade, and by so doing will affect the game's market (just like in the real world). You can also devise

Just a small sampling of the dozens of different types of space stations appearing in the MMORPG game *Eve Online* show how much diversity, creativity, and beauty can be enjoyed via the video-game experience. (Screen shots courtesy of CCP, taken by Richard Abanes during game play.) Interestingly, this game's developer is based in Iceland, as are the online servers to which people from all over the world can connect.

plans with your corporation (or team or guild) to take over certain areas of the game's map by either brute force (as in war) or by political and financial maneuvering.

The undisputed king of MMORPGs is currently *World of Warcraft*, which takes players into a world known as Azeroth, where Orcs, Dwarves, and Elves dwell (it is very Tolkienesque). As of late 2005 this game had three million subscribers. It offers in-game auction houses, pieces of gold a player can use to buy in-game supplies, and a veritable cornucopia of weapons for in-game combat (known as *PvP—player vs. player*). *Leveling*—achievement by a character—can go as high as Level 60.

It is no surprise the demand for such games is increasing as more people become aware of their existence. In fact, in response to that demand, in 2005 Disney released the first MMO that was created specifically for kids and families: *Toontown Online*.

(Other notable MMOs include *City of Heroes, Guild Wars, Dungeons and Dragons Online,* and *Dark Age of Camelot.*)

Real-Time Strategy

Real-Time Strategy (RTS) video games are quite different from RPGs, in that each player, instead of being only one character, exercises control over multiple characters—sometimes dozens, hundreds, and even thousands. Such games usually feature large-scale battles (as well as smaller skirmishes), various armies facing each other, civilizations vying for world supremacy, and immediate responses to tactical decisions made in the moment.

The classic RTS focuses mainly on one's ability to assess resources (for example, an army's numerical strength, the positioning of cities, or rationing of supplies) and then use those resources effectively against an opponent. RTS games often require a fairly advanced level of planning and tactical maneuvering, as well as very quick thinking.

Consider, for example, one of the bestselling and most talked-about real-time strategy games: *Rome: Total War.* You, the player, are able to control tens of thousands of troops and build numerous cities as you lead your forces through both the rise and fall of the Roman Empire. You can control either Roman factions or invading barbarian factions; you can stay on the move or set up camp; you can pillage a town or leave it alone.

Creators of this game have even incorporated into the expanded version the element of religion, which played an extremely significant role in the development and eventual collapse of the Roman Empire. Three faiths are represented for you to choose from: Christianity, Zoroastrianism, and Paganism. You choose how much of the populace of any given city adheres to each faith. The religion with the most adherents becomes that town's main faith. The results can be very interesting:

> The difficulty comes when a city's ruler has a different religion than the city's population. This dramatically increases unrest. In these situations, an influential ruler can eventually convert the population given enough time. Characters can improve their religion influence by wielding powerful holy relics or having monks, teachers, or priests in their retinues. Barring the presence of religious leaders, you'll have to raze buildings associated with the native religion. In their place, you'll erect your own temples, which will slowly bring the people around to seeing things your way.[3]

Other aspects of this striking RTS game include night warfare, crossing rivers with vast armies, unpredictable actions by strong yet disloyal commanders, and hidden characters that will only appear if the conditions are just right (based upon decisions you make). The *Rome: Total War* series is so remarkable, in fact, that the History Channel lifted video footage from its battle scenes to use in the educational program *Time Commanders*.

(Other notable RTS games include *Age of Empires; Command & Conquer; Dragonshard; Warhammer 40K: Dawn of War; Rise of Nations; The Lord of the Rings: The Battle for Middle-Earth 2;* and *Kingdom Under Fire: Heroes.*)

Adventure and Action—Adventure

For those who may want a less stressful game than an RPG or RTS, a good *adventure* title might just be the ticket to hours of entertainment. Such games, in their purest form, involve little fighting or strategizing, but instead focus on solving a mystery or figuring out some way to progress in the game. They often involve a journey, quest, or route of travel that can only be continued as various obstacles are overcome—for example, a seemingly locked door, a mountain with no marked ascent trail, or a pyramid with hidden chambers. In other words, these games are usually plot-driven. (Good examples of adventure games are the *Myst* series and *Escape from Monkey Island.*)

This is not to say that all adventure games avoid serious combat or more mature themes (for example, *Indigo Blue* presents a murder mystery as its central theme). Some adventure games actually have quite a bit of fighting—and a few are rather bloody.

But these latter types are perhaps more properly termed *action–adventure*. They are very similar to basic action games, but they also excel in one-on-one battling.

But action–adventure games add an element of mystery and problem solving to the combat. You do not travel somewhere just to fight, which is the simple essence of action games. Instead, action–adventure usually includes a fairly rich story line—such as the one found in *Shadow of Colossus,* wherein the hero must accomplish various tasks to save his one true love.

Similar action–adventure plots might involve solving a mystery in which you find yourself immersed *(Indigo Blue);* hunting down an evildoer/monster *(Gears of War);* or escaping, surviving, or fighting your way through a very inhospitable situation *(Cold War* and *The Suffering: Ties that Bind).* The action–adventure genre can also be teamed up with the RPG genre to make an action-RPG game (for example, *X-Men Legends 2*).

(Other notable action–adventure games include the *Prince of Persia* series, *Castlevania,* the controversial *Grand Theft Auto* series, *Shadow of the Colossus,* and *The Warriors,* which is based on the 1979 cult film classic by the same title.)

Sports

The *sports* genre of video games encompasses the world of competitive athletic events. Just about every kind of major sport has been transferred into video games (a lot has happened since Atari released *Pong* in 1975). Sport-based games, in fact, are probably the top-selling genre now existing. The following is just a partial list of the many games available:

- Auto-racing—*Nascar 06: Total Team Control; Gran Turismo 4; Enthusia: Professional Racing; Forza Motorsport; Sports Car GT*

- Basketball—*NBA Live 06; NBA 2K6; College Hoops 2K6*

- Baseball—*Major League Baseball 2K5; MVP 06 NCAA Baseball*

- Football—*Madden NFL 06; ESPN NFL 2K5; NCAA Football 2006*

- Soccer—*FIFA Soccer 06; Pro Evolution Soccer 5; World Soccer Winning Eleven 8*

- Hockey—*NHL 06; NHL 2K6; Gretzky NHL '06; ESPN NHL 2K5*

- Skateboarding—*Tony Hawk's Underground 2; Disney Sports Skateboarding; Tony Hawk's American Wasteland; Tony Hawk's Pro Skater 3*

- Wrestling—*WWE SmackDown! vs. Raw 2006; WWE Raw 2*

- Tennis—*Sega Sports Tennis; Top Spin 2; Smash Court Tennis Pro Tournament*

Sports games will undoubtedly continue to be some of the most played games available, especially now that major sports celebrities are lending their name to various titles. And the choice of sports will also be sure to expand. Already we see video games based on sporting events such as fishing *(Pro Cast Sports Fishing)*, powerboat racing *(VR Sports Powerboat Racing)*, cricket *(Cricket 2005)*, and golf *(Tiger Woods PGA Tour 06)*.

Shooters

A *shooter* is a video game in which a player's primary objective is to shoot and kill not only NPCs (nonplaying characters), but also characters being controlled by other players. These are often war-based games, although they also can present a variety of story-line forms. There are basically three kinds of shooters:

- first-person—*Halo, Doom 3, Half-Life 2*
- third-person—*Max Payne, The Punisher*
- online only, which can be either first-person or third-person— *Battlefield 2; Counter Strike: Source; Unreal Tournament 2004;* most recently, *Huxley* (also an MMO)

Shooters that play from a *first-person* perspective let the gamer see the action as if they were the holding the gun and looking forward. A *third-person* shooter, on the other hand, positions the camera angle slightly above and behind the character being controlled in order to give a kind of over-the-shoulder perspective. Both perspectives allow for intense realism, especially with the newer shooters that have been created using high-end graphics. (Examples of such games are *Brothers in Arms: Earned in Blood; Call of Duty 2;* and *F.E.A.R.*, which is arguably the best shooter of 2005.)

To date, some of the most popular first-person shooters have been World War II–based games that serve as a sort of high-tech tribute to the heroes of that global conflict whose sacrifices saved the world from the Axis powers. For instance, *Call of Duty 2: Big Red One* is a tribute to the First Infantry Division of the United States Army, which was celebrated as one of America's

These screen shots from *Advent Rising* (left) and *Soldier of Fortune* (right) show the perspective differences between an "over the shoulder" third-person view and a "down the gunsights" First-Person Shooter (or FPS) view. (Screen shots courtesy of Majesco Games.)

bravest and fiercest fighting groups throughout North Africa, Italy, France, and Germany.

The FPS genre is particularly important in the gaming world because 1) it initiated the whole *professional* gaming segment of the player community; and 2) it brought all players further inside the game via the use of the immediate perspective of first person. The FPS allowed players to actually be part of the game, rather than simply a player controlling an on-screen character.

(Other important shooters include *Return to Castle Wolfenstein, Serious Sam 2*, and *Timesplitters*.)

Platform Games

If you have ever played a *Mario Brothers* game, *Donkey Kong, The Legend of Zelda*, or any other game that has that straight-across-the-screen, two-dimensional look, then you have played a *platform* game. These games helped kick-start the whole video-game craze back in the mid-1980s. They are often very family-friendly and can provide hours of entertainment for both young and old alike (my mother, who is 70 years old, plays nothing but platform games—go, Mom!).

Platform games also tend to be simple to understand. Consequently, they are perfect for young kids or new gamers. The player controls only a single character that pretty much just runs across the screen from left to right (and right to left) in an effort to sidestep objects, duck projectiles, and leap across chasms. A player's character can also climb ladders (or ropes/vines), run through caverns, and swim underwater—all in an effort to get to the next level or receive some bonus prize (like tasty treats or health/energy "marbles"). The best of these games might be described as very, very cute.

(Other popular platform games include *The Lion King, Congo Bongo, Spider-Man,* and *Teenage Mutant Ninja Turtles.*)

God Games

Some of the most fascinating video games fall into the *god games* category. These are usually multiple-genre hybrids that include features associated with role-playing, action, and adventure. Such games (for example, *Dungeon Keeper, Populous,* and to some extent *The Sims* series of games) enable a player to take on the role of controlling the world being observed (or played in).

The popularity of such games seems to validate, at least to some extent, the view of Christian author J.R.R. Tolkien, renowned creator of The Lord of the Rings. He theorized that because all of us are created in God's image (Genesis 2), we ourselves have been imbued with the ability (and desire) to create. But we can only do so via the creation of fantasy worlds (or "sub-creations"). He believed that these worlds showed a kind of primal urge in everyone; a part of our very nature. All humans are endowed with this predilection, albeit some to a greater extent than others.

One video game that dramatically illustrates Tolkien's thoughts is the up-and-coming *Spore* by the creator of *The Sims*. *Spore* starts out by giving players a portion of microscopic "goo" that you must develop into a more complex organism. You can then evolve your organism further along to create almost any kind of life form. You can add a myriad of features. Eventually you see what other online players are creating:

> You develop brainpower, and you move from single creatures to tribes. Then you build fire. Then you give them sticks and spears. Then they fight....Now you build cities. And you zoom out and see other cities....Now you're fighting other civilizations....Now you can build a UFO and zoom out and see other planets. You can terraform new worlds. You can plant colonies....You can zoom out further and see other galaxies and systems.... Fellow gamers will be your predators, or your allies.[4]

Another game worthy of note is *Black & White 2*. It casts each player "as an omniscient overseer of an island populated with young civilizations."[5] The game allows a player to not just create a world, but to create a world that is directly affected by yet another creation of yours—a *creature avatar* (a kind of pet animal that acts not only as an on-screen representative of you, but also behaves in ways that, according to how you "raise" it, directly influence the game):

You can teach your creature to play and entertain villages, help build and expand towns and even lead your armies….It's possible to move through most of the game as a peaceful deity, conquering the hearts and minds of nearby populations by building spectacular, bustling cities filled with happy citizens. Or you might whip your townsfolk (literally) into huge armies and mercilessly conquer other towns, perhaps using your creature as a pacifier in order to calm villagers after you've terrorized them into submission.[6]

Such a game almost necessitates talk among players about right and wrong, good and evil, and related ethical–moral issues. As with so many of today's video games, the choices made by players affect how the game both plays and ends—sort of like real life. There is no reason why a game like *Black & White 2* could not spawn deep philosophical conversation groups wherein such topics as mercy, justice, forgiveness, and kindness are analyzed through the eyes of players and the worlds they have created.

Perhaps one day such things will be the case. But for now there is still a great deal of controversy surrounding video games. This is especially true of the ratings that have been given to games, Hollywood's involvement with the gaming industry, and problems surrounding the exposure of children to games clearly intended for mature players only. These issues will be the focus of chapter 2.

2
The Ratings Game

[Video games are] like books, films, the internet,
or any other medium. All can be used to depict sex and
violence, or to educate and inform. Indeed the inclusion
of violent and sexual content in games is arguably a sign of the
maturity of the medium, as games become more like films.

—"CHASING THE DREAM"
The Economist

Few people realize just how closely intertwined the video-game industry and Hollywood have become. Their relatively new alliance is due in part to the money-making potential of video-game/Hollywood joint projects. Hollywood, of course, has always been a lucrative industry. But now that the combined revenue of game software and hardware is edging out Hollywood box-office revenue (not including DVD sales), video games are quickly emerging as a consistent source of inspiration for movie moguls. There is now, in fact, "widespread collaboration across industries, with Hollywood art directors, science fiction novelists, and alternative musicians all working on games."[1]

This collaboration started as far back as the 1982 movie *Tron,* which introduced a whole generation to not only the wonders of computer games, but also the use of computer graphics in films. The relationship between the video-game industry and Hollywood developed gradually until the late 1990s and on, when the release pace of video-game-to-movie and movie-to-video-game projects accelerated.* Examples of the former would be the *Lara Croft: Tomb Raider* films and the *Resident Evil* series, while examples of the latter would be the *Indiana Jones* and the *Star Wars* games.

As of late 2005 dozens of video-game movie projects had either just been completed or were getting started. This cross-pollination between video games and Hollywood will undoubtedly continue, especially as more celebrities begin viewing involvement with video games as a major plus to their careers and bank accounts. Several stars have already been involved in major motion pictures based on video games. Professional-wrestler-turned-actor Dwayne "The Rock" Johnson, for example, was featured in *Doom.* And the science fiction adventure film *Aeon Flux* starred Hollywood A-lister Charlize Theron, whose voice and likeness were also used in the video game.

Numerous celebrities, in fact, are now involved in video-game production—as are several famous directors, who are getting into the act by using their talents to help mold video games into a cohesive, dynamic, and well-executed experience (see sidebar). And star-studded casts are only a microcosm of what is happening

---

* See also pages 82–85 in regard to connections between Hollywood and game development for the armed forces.

elsewhere in the video-game industry, which now regularly calls upon well-known celebrities. The work has become so common that "it's rare to play a big-budget video game in 2005 without seeing at least a few famous names roll by in the opening credits."[2]

Actors and Directors in Video Games

Voice-overs for the new shoot-'em-up videogame *GUN* will feature a host of movie stars including composer/actor Kris Kristofferson (*A Star is Born, Alice Doesn't Live Here Anymore*); Lance Henriksen (*Aliens, Millennium* TV series); Ron Perlman (TV's *Beauty and the Beast* series); and Tom Skerritt (*Top Gun, Contact*). Voice-overs for the game *True Crime: New York City* spotlight the acting skills of several megastars, including Mickey Rourke, Laurence Fishburne, and Christopher Walken.

Just a few of the directors involved in video-game projects include Marcus Nispel (*Alice*); John Singleton and David Lynch (*Enter the Matrix*); George Romero (*City of the Dead*); Christophe Gans (*Silent Hill*); and Uwe Boll (with multiple games to films—*Far Cry, Dungeon Siege*, and *BloodRayne*, to name but a few). Video games to movies in development as of late 2005 included several of those just mentioned: *BloodRayne, Max Payne*, and *Alice* (a dark and twisted version of *Alice in Wonderland* starring Sarah Michelle Gellar of *Buffy the Vampire Slayer* fame).

Classic tales were not forgotten at the 2005 IGN conference. *Star Wars* was prominently featured not only through video games, but also via roaming characters from the blockbuster films. The event went so far as to hold a "light saber" battle between Jedi warriors (right). It was all very entertaining—until I was momentarily taken prisoner by two Imperial stormtroopers and given a citation for carrying an unlicensed camera and having no permit from the "Empire" to take photos. (Photos: Richard Abanes.)

The movie *Halo* (to be released by Universal/20th Century Fox in 2007) promises to be one of the best transferences yet of a video game to the silver screen. The script is to be written by Alex Garland *(28 Days Later)*, and its executive producer will be Peter Jackson, whose reputation was forever solidified after his work as director/producer of *The Lord of the Rings* movie trilogy. Jackson also directed the 2005 hit *King Kong* while using his creative talents to mold the video game released under that same classic title.

Video games and movies have clearly joined forces to present the public with a smorgasboard of entertainment choices that appeal to numerous crossover audiences. One inevitable result of this interaction has been influence; that is, influence of the movie industry on the gaming industry. The undeniable fact is that video games have progressively become more and more like movies. They now include mature themes, with varying levels of violence, sex, and even illicit drug use. Consequently, like movies, video games are rated.

Choosing Wisely

Computer and video games are the future of entertainment, and Hollywood knows it. Although book sales have dropped and movie theater attendance has risen only slightly, as we've noted previously, the electronic gaming industry is exploding. In 2004 Americans spent an unprecedented $7.3 billion on computer and video games.[3]

This upsurge in popularity may be due to the fact that any game consumer can now get the best of all worlds. Digital and film technologies have become so similar to each other that the realism of electronic games has finally approached that of movies. Director Naresh Hirani, for instance, "drew on the film world and used the cinematic techniques of the film world" in creating his game *The Getaway: Black Monday*. He and other game developers "see a convergence of the kind of experience we're offering with the kind of experience the film world is offering."[4]

Problems have thus arisen in regard to content. To help those who may be concerned about exposing children to material that is too mature for them, the Entertainment Software Ratings

Board (ESRB) was created in 1994 by the Entertainment Software Association (ESA).[5] It is no small task that the ESRB faces each year, given its responsibility to assign more than 1000 ratings annually. It currently uses six ratings (which is more than the number of movie ratings currently in use—G, PG, PG-13, R, and NC-17). The system is as follows:[6]

- *AO*, Adults Only, has "content that should only be played by persons 18 years and older." This rating is for games that "may include prolonged scenes of intense violence and/or graphic sexual content and nudity."

- *M*, Mature, is intended for persons 17 and older. "Titles in this category may contain intense violence, blood and gore, sexual content and/or strong language."

- *T*, Teen, is deemed suitable for kids 13 and older. These games may "contain violence, suggestive themes, crude humor, minimal blood and/or infrequent use of strong language."

- *E 10+*, Everyone 10+, is supposed to be appropriate for children 10 and older. Such games may include "more cartoon violence, fantasy or mild violence, mild language, and/or minimal suggestive themes."

- *E*, Everyone, contains material "suitable for ages 6 and older." Nevertheless, these games might include "minimal cartoon, fantasy or mild violence and/or infrequent use of mild language."

- *EC*, Early Childhood, are games "suitable for ages 3 and older" and would contain "no material that parents would find inappropriate."

Any of these ratings may be applied to a computer or

video game based on its content. By way of comparison, an M-rated game might best be equated to an R-rated film, while a T-rated game would correspond to a PG-13 film. But these ratings comprise only the "age appropriateness" part of the rating. The second part of the rating goes a step further, detailing the actual contents of the game to leave no doubt about what might be objectionable to some players (and parents). This second tier of ratings includes 32 different descriptors:[7]

- *Alcohol reference:* reference to and/or images of alcohol beverages
- *Animated blood:* discolored and/or unrealistic depictions of blood
- *Blood:* depictions of blood
- *Blood and gore:* depictions of blood or the mutilation of body parts
- *Crude humor:* depictions of dialogue involving vulgar antics, including "bathroom" humor
- *Drug reference:* reference to and/or images of illegal drugs
- *Edutainment:* content of product provides user with specific skills development or reinforcement learning within an entertainment setting; skill development is an integral part of product
- *Fantasy violence:* violent actions of a fantasy nature, involving human or nonhuman characters in situations easily distinguishable from real life
- *Informational:* overall content of product is data, facts, resource information, reference materials or instructional text

- *Intense violence:* graphic and realistic-looking depictions of physical conflict; may involve extreme and/or realistic blood, gore, weapons, and depictions of human injury and death
- *Language:* mild to moderate use of profanity
- *Lyrics:* mild references to profanity, sexuality, violence, alcohol, or drug use in music
- *Mature humor:* depictions or dialogue involving "adult" humor, including several sexual references
- *Mild violence:* mild scenes depicting characters in unsafe and/or violent situations
- *Nudity:* graphic or prolonged depictions of nudity
- *Partial nudity:* brief and/or mild depictions of nudity
- *Real gambling:* player can gamble, including betting or wagering real cash or currency
- *Sexual themes:* mild to moderate sexual references and/or depictions; may include partial nudity
- *Sexual violence:* depictions of rape or other sexual acts
- *Simulated gambling:* player can gamble without betting or wagering real cash or currency
- *Some adult assistance may be needed:* intended for very young ages
- *Strong language:* explicit and/or frequent use of profanity
- *Suggestive themes:* mild provocative references or materials
- *Tobacco reference:* reference to and/or images of tobacco products
- *Use of drugs:* the consumption or use of illegal drugs
- *Use of alcohol:* the consumption of alcoholic beverages

- *Use of tobacco:* the consumption of tobacco products
- *Violence:* scenes involving aggressive conflict

However, in the same way that content varies from movie to movie, so too does content vary from game to game. In other words, one video game may have more profanity than another game of the same rating—just like one PG-13 movie might have more swearing in it than another PG-13 movie. This becomes especially dicey with online game-playing, which brings into a player's experiences the dialogue of real-life players from all over the world. Consequently, the ESRB also places a qualifier on every game's rating: "Game Experience May Change During Online Play."

Can I See Your ID?

The rating system used by the ESRB is a very helpful tool that can be used to determine the appropriateness of video games for children, as well as teens and even adults. But the system does not always work as intended, nor is it always precise. For example, *Return to Castle Wolfenstein: Platinum Edition* is rated M for "Blood and gore" and "Violence." In my opinion, however, the descriptor "Violence" should be "Intense violence" because the game includes realistic "weapons, and depictions of human injury and death." Similarly, the sophisticated war game *Battlefield 2* is rated only T despite its extremely realistic war scenarios and depictions of weapons and the death of soldiers. It, too, mentions only "Violence."

Both of these games were able to escape the "Intense Violence" descriptor simply because there is no significant amount of realistically rendered blood. In other words, the soldiers get shot and die, but no blood is visible. The same can be said about the T-rated first-person shooter *Medal of Honor* (a World War II game). But even a reviewer in *Computer Gaming* notes, "This has always baffled me, this idea that a game that involves the player gunning down literally thousands of soldiers is appropriate for kids because no one bleeds. (It's arguably more dangerous to never show consequences of violence.)"[8]

In other words, some computer games might be rated lower than they should be. This drawback of the system, however, is only one problem. A far more widespread and serious issue that must be addressed is how some retailers are not abiding by the rating codes and regularly sell games to children and teens that are intended for older players.

The ESRB ratings have gone virtually unheeded for years by untold numbers of retailers, and as a result, many children have been engaging in game play unsuitable for them (based on the rating system). Game manufacturers know and admit as much. The game *Diablo 2,* for instance, an M-rated release, is indeed being played by under-17 kids, according to Mike Morhaime, president of the company that makes the game.[9]

This is not uncommon. In 2003, several Seattle-area "14-and 15-year-old members of Students Against Violence Everywhere (SAVE) put retailers to the test" by trying to purchase games supposedly not for them. "Twelve of 13 stores sold M-rated games to underage students." [10] The games purchased included soft pornography, profanity, and intense violence. But that was not the worst of it:

SAVE's most astonishing case arose when a member was returning a game after a successful purchase. When the student said she had to return the game because her mother would not allow her to have it, a store employee suggested the underage student should have "just lied to (her) parents and told them that the game was about entomology or something."[11]

According to Dr. David Walsh, author of *Selling Out America's Children*, "Violent entertainment is aimed at children because it is profitable. Questions of right or wrong, beneficial or harmful, are not considered. The only question is 'Will it sell?'" This is indeed a key issue given the fact that in 2004, "'T' and 'M' sales accounted for 54 percent of overall sales."[12] There is simply too much money to be made off of M-rated games for some retailers to care about who is laying down the cash.

Moreover, selling M-rated games to kids is not illegal. Because the guidelines are voluntary, some retailers choose to not heed them. In 2004, for example, The National Institute on Media and the Family "did a secret shopper survey in 12 states and found that 50 percent of boys and 8 percent of girls were able to buy 'Mature,' or M-rated, games."[13] In other words, if a child finds a store willing to sell them M-rated games, then they have full access to the worst of the worst depictions of sex and violence.[14]

The failure of retailers to enforce ratings is only one problem facing the gaming industry. A far more pervasive hindrance to the efficacy of video-game ratings is parental indifference. Parents (and others) have earned a reputation among gamers as being utterly oblivious to video-game basics, such as what the ratings mean. Some kids, for instance, are telling their gullible parents that "M" actually stands for either "Minors" or "Mild," and in this way, they are gaining access to Mature games.

But this is not the fault of the video-game industry, because the large "M" on the video-game box actually reads "MATURE." To know the rating of a game, all one has to do is look at the cover. Too many parents, it seems, simply do not care enough about the issue to get involved. As one Wal-Mart worker explained in a letter to *Official PlayStation Magazine*, when parents are told that the game they are about to purchase is "Mature," they respond about "80 percent of the time" by simply saying, "Oh well, they see worse on TV."[15]

Fortunately, some parents do pay attention to the ratings and take responsibility over what their kids play. It must also be noted that gaming magazines, for the most part, have sought to support the ratings as much as possible. For example, in response to a kid who wrote *GamePro* magazine to complain about his father taking away his M-rated *Resident Evil 4* game, the magazine's editors replied,

> If you're not at least 17, then as your parent, Dad's responsible for determining what's appropriate for you. You might at least preserve your gameplaying privileges by showing him you respect the fact that he's just trying to look out for you and that there are non-M-rated games you enjoy playing, too. You do enjoy playing some non-M games, right?[16]

But some politicians, morality groups, and antigaming activists have not responded to the problems so calmly or rationally. Instead, they have sought to enact laws to "protect children." The reactions to these proposals by dedicated gamers (and casual players) have not, generally speaking, been positive. Truth be told, many of their objections are valid.

Playing Politics

The legal and political war between the video-game industry and the antigaming public reached a new level of intensity in 2005, when Illinois governor Rod Blagojevich signed a law to "regulate the purchase of violent and sexually explicit video games by minors."[17] Although the legislation did not prohibit the creation or *general* sale of video games, it did put M-rated games into a category of regulated products similar to cigarettes, alcohol, and pornography.

California governor Arnold Schwarzenegger signed a similar law, which created "a penalty of up to $1,000 for any retailer who's caught selling games that depict extreme acts of violence to buyers under 18 years of age." The governor's move barred "the sale and rental to minors of games that show such things as the killing, maiming or sexual assault of a character depicted as human, and which are determined to be especially heinous, atrocious or cruel."[18]

Governor Jennifer Granholm of Michigan had previously taken the same kind of action by signing several bills that prohibited selling to minors not only sexually explicit games, but also "ultra-violent explicit video games" (under penalty of $5,000). By "ultra-violent," Michigan's law meant any game that "continually and repetitively depicts extreme and loathsome violence." Such violence was further defined as follows:

> Real or simulated graphic depictions of physical inju-
> ries or physical violence against parties who realistically
> appear to be human beings, including actions causing
> death, inflicting cruelty, dismemberment, decapitation,
> maiming, disfigurement, or other mutilation of body
> parts, murder, criminal sexual conduct, or torture.

The problem with such laws, however, is that the definitions behind them are too vague. And it is upon this premise that the Entertainment Software Association has filed lawsuits against all of the aforementioned statutes. As of late 2005, similar legal challenges had already been successfully mounted against restrictive video-game laws in the state of Washington, the city of Indianapolis, and St. Louis County, Missouri.

As of late 2005 it was being predicted that all similar laws would eventually be nullified or revoked one by one. Why? The laws as they now stand on the books in California, Michigan, and Illinois do not help anyone adhere to the ESRB ratings. None of them clearly state something like, "Fines will be levied upon any retailers selling M-rated games to children below the ESRB-recommended 17-plus age limit." That would be as easily enforceable as restrictions against tobacco products and pornography. Instead, for some reason, the stipulations of each measure force retailers to figure out for themselves what kind of violent action in a game is, for example, "especially heinous, atrocious, or cruel."

Hal Halprin, president of the Interactive Entertainment Merchants Association, has correctly noted that these laws "make retailers responsible for determining what would be an unacceptable level of violence in a game and then enforcing carding policies inhibiting the sale of those games to minors." However, he goes on to note, "the wording of the laws is vague and difficult to discern."[19] In other words, as these laws now stand, a 15-year-old might not be able to buy *Grand Theft Auto* or *The Punisher* at his neighborhood Target, but he would be able to buy it at a Game-Stop only ten miles away at the megamall. Why? Because that particular retailer simply has a different definition from Target of an "especially heinous, atrocious, or cruel" video game.

It is indeed possible that some kind of legislation needs to be enacted that will safeguard children and teens by preventing them from purchasing video games beyond their age group. But more precise wording and more careful thought must go into any such law. Currently, however, non-game-playing politicians seem interested only in taking yet another controversial issue and using it to further their own political agenda.

The Culture Clash

A major problem seems to be that most of the politicians and antigaming pundits have never actually played a video game for any significant period of time—let alone experienced the thrill of mastering the increasingly difficult levels of a game or joining an online multiplayer match with others from all over the world. This ignorance of electronic entertainment in general, not to mention specific details, helps no one. In fact, it actually harms fruitful dialogue and confuses the issue.

California Assemblyman Leland Yee, for example, got many of his facts jumbled when seeking to convince his state of video-game dangers. In condemning the ESRB, Yee stated, "Whether it is *JFK: Reloaded, Manhunt, 25 to Life,* or now *Grand Theft Auto,* the video-game industry continues to demonstrate a sense of arrogance toward public opinion and a lack of responsibility in protecting our children."[20] But *JFK: Reloaded* was an *online-only* game. As such, it never even had an ESRB rating because it did not fall under ESRB jurisdiction. And when Yee made his remark, *25 to Life* had not yet even been released.[21]

And then we have the infamous—at least to gamers—Jack Thompson, a Florida attorney who seems committed to making video games sound as bad as possible, usually in direct contradiction of the facts. For example, in a tirade against *The Sims 2,* Thompson alleged that a special code entered during game play could remove the pixelation used to blur body parts of otherwise nude characters (for example, when they shower). He decried the game, telling shocked listeners that entry of the code revealed "full-frontal nudity, including nipples, penises, labia, and pubic hair." He even said pedophiles would delight in it because the code also worked on child characters in the game, which in turn would allow such criminals to "rehearse" real molestation.[22]

Thompson, however, has apparently never played *The Sims 2* (with or without the code). Had he done so, he would have seen that beneath the blurring lies nothing except smooth, skin-tone coloring (imagine an unclothed mannequin in a nearby department store). EA Games vice president Jeff Brown observed, "It's like looking at Barbie and Ken [dolls]."[23]

Mr. Thompson has been just as sensationalistic about video-game violence, arguing that it is akin to the pornography that serial murderer Ted Bundy relished. Video-game violence "is not a release of aggression. It is a training for aggression,"[24] declared

Thompson. But again, his knowledge in this area is severely lacking. There have been numerous studies that show a wide variety of results with regard to this complex issue of human behavior. (For more on this, see the next chapter.)

Unfortunately, non-game-playing politicians and attorneys are only part of the problem. As we noted earlier, most mainstream journalists do not seem to be gamers either. Thus they have little to no understanding of how gamers play, why they play, or what benefits they gain from playing. And simply *explaining* today's far more technologically mature video games doesn't go very far in illuminating for nonplayers the vast differences between them and the kiddie games of yesteryear (such as *Super Mario Brothers, Mike Tyson's Punch-Out*, or *The Legend of Zelda*). Many journalists, as a result, cover video games with a biased eye against them and resort to their own form of sensationalism for the sake of a good story.

The only way a person can really understand current video games is to experience some of the best ones today's industry can offer. Otherwise, as one *Computer Gaming World* article put it, "it's like trying to describe the difference between the colors red and blue to a blind person."[25] And getting facts straight is important too.

For example, there has been a great deal of controversy and outrage over the plethora of M-rated video games. But the truth is, only about 12 percent of the games released in 2005 were M-rated (although it could be argued that perhaps a few more of them *should* have received the "Mature" stamp). That percentage is a relatively small segment of the overall video-game market. Most games are either T-rated or E-rated. And interestingly, as we saw in chapter 1, the largest segment of games purchased falls into the sports genre.

All the foregoing is not to say that there are no negative aspects of video games. Parents, educators, church leaders, and even politicians do have a legitimate concern about how some video games might affect some children under some circumstances. And M-rated and AO-rated games, of course, should not even be in the hands of children. But as we have seen, such restrictions are not always possible, given the lax attitude of many retailers and, unfortunately, some parents. But what exactly might one find in the more mature games, and what have studies shown about their effects on people? The next two chapters will examine these questions.

3
Mature Means Mature, Part One

Video games are this generation's rock 'n' roll; they're this generation's lifestyle interest. They're culturally relevant, but they're not really understood by their parents, their teachers, their congressmen. They're the new popular, cultural forum for this generation.

CHARLES HIRSCHHORN
founder/CEO, G4 Television

The most talked-about controversy that has hit the video-game industry grabbed worldwide headlines in June 2005. Patrick Wildenborg, a video-game code hacker (known as a *modder*) stumbled upon some hidden and unused code in *Grand Theft Auto: San Andreas* (a thug-themed action–adventure role-playing game developed by the company Rockstar). The code allowed players to "unlock" a sexually explicit minigame in which players could make their screen characters engage in graphic sex acts!

Computer owners could unlock the unregistered content via the now-infamous "Hot Coffee" *mod* (modification), available on the Internet. Owners of a console version of the game (for example, Playstation 2) were able to unveil the previously invisible content via a series of codes that simply needed to be entered into the program through some third-party software program (for example, GameShark).

A media circus ensued. Commentators on every network decried the destructive nature of video games. The U.S. House of Representatives began investigating Rockstar to see if it had "deliberately misled the [software] ratings board" in order to receive a Mature rating as opposed to the more restrictive Adults Only rating. Ripples of controversy even hit Australian shores, where the government's Office of Film and Literature Classification revoked the game's MA15+ rating while issuing a directive for businesses to remove the game from their shelves.[1]

Not only was the game pulled from stores in Australia, but many of the largest retailers in America stopped selling it, especially after it was issued a new rating—Adults Only—by the Entertainment Software Ratings Board. This action demonstrated how swiftly the ESRB moved to correct the never-before-seen problem. Entertainment Software Association president Doug Lowenstein explained,

> This is the first time in 11 years that there has been anything even remotely similar to this….People can trust the system and rely on these ratings….The ESRB has made it clear that companies must disclose all content that is on a disk that is going to ship whether it is playable content or not.[2]

Nonetheless, anti-video-game attorney Jack Thompson of

Florida went so far as to denounce the ESA—the main lobbying group for video games—as a "criminal" organization. He even referred to ESA president Lowenstein as a "highly-paid thug." But Thompson's political grandstanding and over-the-top accusations hardly addressed the real issue: that a single game developer had foolishly and wrongfully "misled the ESRB (and by extension the public) about what content was on the CD" of *Grand Theft Auto*.[3]

The game's publisher, Take Two, responded by stopping the game's production and promising to release a new version sans the hidden code. But Take Two was already looking at a possible loss of $80 million in sales for the unwise programming stunt pulled by Rockstar, which in turn ended up losing perhaps $50 million in revenue. Many gamers—both hard-core and casual—considered the whole "hidden code" affair a serious error of judgment that did nothing but hurt the public image of video games. Even ESA president Lowenstein made what seemed to be a not-so-subtle criticism of Rockstar when, at a 2005 gaming conference, he stated that perhaps not everything that *could* be done in video games *should* be done in them.[4]

Under the Radar

So how did the game developer respond to the controversy? Not particularly well. It was reported, for instance, that a Rockstar spokesperson actually denied the code existed in the "game discs manufactured by Rockstar or its agents." Later, the company changed its tune, admitting that the material was present but could only be accessed via "intentional and significant technical modifications." Rockstar, in other words, blamed the modder (Patrick Wildenborg) for its woes, saying that the game's controversial content was "the work of a determined group of hackers who have gone to significant trouble to alter scenes in the official version of the game."[5]

But the modding of games has become all but expected. In fact, the producers and players of video games wait expectantly to see what things modders will unlock or tweak in the coding (used and unused) within a video game's matrix. Rockstar deliberately left the code in the game and would have to have been very naïve to think that it would not be discovered rather quickly.

To make matters worse, the now-notorious game developer went forward with plans to release a new game titled *Bully*—a game "set in a reform school, where you have to fight back against bullying pupils and cruel teachers."[6] This prompted only more public outrage, given the fact that Rockstar also just happens to be the developer of the very disturbing (and controversial) game *Manhunt*, recognized as one of the most gruesome games in recent years.

As a result of Rockstar's apparent effort to garner a reputation for being the maker of ultraviolent and sexually explicit games, the whole gaming industry is being tarred and feathered with the label "OFFENSIVE." This has led many gamers interested in the future of the industry to begin saying, "Hey, all of you game developers who are trying to see how far you can push the envelope—CUT IT OUT!"[7]

Rockstar, however, is not the only company to include hidden code in games. Such code, for example, exists in the highly popular *Medal of Honor* (developer—Electronic Arts), a World

War II–based shooter game that received a Teen rating because, although rather violent, it contains no blood—no blood that can be seen. But a quick download from the Internet of yet another mod makes the blood visible in "all of its crimson glory. Had Electronic Arts shipped this 'bloody' version, it's highly likely it would have received a 'Mature' rating."[8] *Computer Games* magazine rightly commented that such shenanigans

> undermine the spirit of the ESRB and give the illusion that developers and publishers have little regard for the ratings....Making it easy for mods like this will do nothing but draw even more unwanted attention from showboating lawmakers trying to score points in the culture wars....In this case *[Grand Theft Auto]*, people have every right to be upset....Hiding the "adult" and "mature" content as a way to avoid scrutiny from the ratings board—or just to be funny or cool—is neither adult or mature, or funny or cool for that matter. It only shows the immaturity of the people making and publishing the games....The industry is desperate to be taken more seriously; however, if it really wants to sit at the adult table, it needs to act like a grown-up and not a pimply teenager.[9]

Such issues are only a small part of the problems associated with video games. In many "M" games there can be found an intense level of brutality, mayhem, murder, glorification of crime, and even torture. Overt sexuality, sexual references, or both can also be found in a significant number of mature games, along with partial (or near-full) nudity and sexual themes.

Most disturbing is how these games, though rated M, are being marketed to children who should not even being playing such games, according to the ESRB. This was discovered by a Federal Trade Commission study, which showed that about 70 percent of M-rated games, in fact, are being marketed directly to kids under 17.[10] This is troubling, given some of the seriously mature content of M-rated games and the fact that even some T-rated games could justifiably be rated with M.

Welcome to the Dark Side

It must be stressed at this point that Mature games are intended for mature players. Care must be taken to restrict these games from those for whom they were not intended. And that is the job of parents, child-care workers, educators, the ESRB, game producers, and members of the video-game industry. As previously mentioned, there are a wide variety of games for children that few parents would find objectionable. Others, nonetheless, contain material worth exploring and understanding. And it's wise to note that the darker and more disturbing aspects of video games can appear in just about any genre: shooter, RPG, action, even sports.

Perhaps the most problematic games are shooters. These games commonly, though not always, present realistic killing, brutality, and extreme gore (for example, the splattering of blood, guts, and body parts). Such images could certainly be damaging to at least *some* children's and teens' minds and emotions. What makes shooters so potentially harmful (and also so very involving and intense from a mature gamer's standpoint) is how the action occurs with the scenes unfolding as if the player were himself or herself looking at the environment—usually down the barrel of a weapon. You get a far more realistic experience of shooting or killing an opponent (either an NPC or another real-world player).

Action titles also lend themselves to a fair amount of bloodshed and mature imagery. So often, in fact, is this the case, that the mature aspects of such games have become a major selling point for them. Consider the words of Jean-Christophe Guyot—creative director of the TPS *Prince of Persia 2: Warrior Within*—who explained in 2004 how his team designed their M-rated game using a "brand new fighting system" that allowed for "grabs, decapitations, and strangulations" to be executed in gruesome combinations.[11]

> [You] start with a grab, and then decide whether you want to throw the enemy at another one, slice him, strangulate him, or stab a sword through his body....We also wanted to give game players a new sense of power.... For instance, [there is] a double sword decapitation. For this move we put a lot of effort into the richness of the animations; special effects like slow motion and camera angles to make it absolutely memorable.[12]

This kind of boasting about multiple ways of killing, maiming, and obliterating foes reflects the way in which many M-rated game makers appeal to potential buyers. They *must* make their games stand out amid a crowded arena. For example, one of the most horrific games, far worse than *Prince of Persia*, is *The Punisher*, which incorporates a new element into the violent mix: torture.

In *The Punisher*, gamers get to play the role of Frank Castle, a man who embarks on his murderous exploits in hope of vengeance. He is searching for his nemesis, and to get more information, he

Screen shots from two of the newest and most controversial video games on the market: *Hitman 2* (left) and *25 Years to Life* (right). Both titles fall into the "realistic crime" genre and prominently feature murder—complete with blood-spattered walls and floors. They are ultrarealistic. (Screen shots courtesy of Eidos Games.)

must apprehend others and "interrogate" them until they talk. Video clips of real game play available on the Internet as of 2005 included some horrifying scenes:

- *Clip 1:* Frank slowly shoves a man, feet first, into a tree-branch shredder.

- *Clip 2:* Frank viciously smashes a man's face into cement by stomping down on the back of his head until it splits open, thus killing him.

- *Clip 3:* Frank incinerates a man alive by locking him in a crema-tion oven.

Yet another clip (only a minute in length) shows a room full of men being machine-gunned to death (complete with explod-ing heads and torsos), one man getting knifed through the top of his head, another having his throat slashed, and another being blown up after getting shoved into a closed coffin with a live grenade that explodes—all topped off with four profanities that were shouted during the segment.[13]

From Bad to Worse

As vivid as *The Punisher* is, it is not the worst of the games out there. *Postal 2: Share the Pain* goes several steps further. Unlike *The Punisher*, which directs its violence only at criminals, *Postal 2* calls for the gamer to viciously and unmercifully attack innocent people. The game actually encourages the player to be sadistic, with pop-up directives such as "Hit 'Q' to open doors and kick people in the face. It's fun."[14]

The single goal in this particular FPS is to wander around town causing as much mayhem as possible by murdering everyone. And if you merely wound someone, they fall to their knees and beg for mercy, saying things like "Spare me, I have kids" and "Please, don't kill me." Of course, you can still opt to murder them in cold blood. If you choose to electrically shock them with a Taser gun, they will writhe in agony, foam at the mouth, and say things such as "I can't breathe" or "I can't feel my legs." You can then kill them at your leisure—or urinate on them.

Postal 2 even gives motivation to kill by having other characters antagonize you. Some, if bumped on the street, will say things like "Hey, watch it" and "Idiot!" Then, if you kick them, bash them with a shovel, or wound them with a bullet to the leg, they fall into a pleading position, crying out, "I'm sorry, so very sorry," just before they start begging for their life. You are expected to kill them. And for good measure, you can pour gasoline on their body and set them alight with the flick of a match.

Equally harsh are the screams of terror and the background dialogue echoing around you (the shooter) while you wander through town. These lines are frighteningly reminiscent of what a teen might hear either *while* engaging in a Columbine-like killing spree or *after* doing so. The exclamations include, "He seemed like such a nice quiet boy," "This can't be happening," and "Somebody make it stop!"

After only a few short minutes the town is full of blood and bodies, terrorized citizens are screaming as they flee from you, and assorted police officers are in hot pursuit. If everything gets too intense or it looks like the police may capture you, there are two choices: 1) surrender, which will get you arrested and taken to a jail from which you must try to escape; or 2) press "K" and commit suicide—yes, commit suicide.

If you press "K," the camera angle is suddenly no longer first-person. The view is turned around so you can see your character. He is dressed exactly like the Columbine high-school killers (a black trenchcoat and dark sunglasses). You can then either zoom in closer, or zoom out, to get a better look at yourself. If you subsequently choose to do the unthinkable, just hit the space bar. Your character boldly declares, "I regret nothing." Then he blows himself up with a grenade he places in his mouth.

Sadly, the developers of *Postal 2* also use their game to mock concerns about game violence. For instance, a newspaper your character can pick up says, "A New Arcade Game Promises Homelessness Training for Kids: Town Council Decries Lurid Video, Nobody Cares." As you read, your character's thoughts are heard: "Man, what those game developers won't do for a buck. At least it's educational." Also, after you commit suicide, if you

These screenshots from the FPS *Postal 2: Share the Pain* show the graphic nature of the game. The sole objective of this title is to kill, kill, kill—often in ways that are not just brutal, but sadistic. Using a handgun to murder women out for a stroll (top left) quickly escalates to killing police officers with a fully automatic assault rifle (top right).

The player can even immolate his victims using a can of gasoline and matches he carries around (bottom left). Or, he can simply use a shotgun to massacre his victims (bottom right). Keyboard controls in this horrific game even allow the onscreen "shooter" to urinate on his murdered victims. (Screen shots by Richard Abanes, courtesy of Running With Scissors).

allow the game to keep running, people start congregating around your body to chat, often saying, "Somebody call Lieberman," and "I blame *Doom*."

The first remark is a reference to Senator Joseph Lieberman who, in his efforts to protect young minds, has been trying to prohibit by law the marketing of mature entertainment forms (for example, movies and games) to children.[15] He also helped create the Entertainment Software Board Rating System. Consequently, he is often vilified by "computer and video game players for his stance on video games; he is a strong supporter of video game censorship."[16]

The second comment seems to make fun of concerns voiced after the 1999 Columbine high-school massacre. *Doom* is not just another ultraviolent video game—it is the same game Columbine killer Eric Harris mentioned in the chilling pre-attack video he made with Dylan Klebold. He said that what was about to befall Columbine was "going to be like" *Doom*.[17] Apparently, the violence issue is all just a big joke to the makers of *Postal 2* and to various other game developers, who deride all warnings about the content of their games.

All in Good Fun?

Numerous video-game producers brazenly play up the violence factor with such advertising one-liners as these gems: "It's only as violent as you are" *(Postal 2: Share the Pain);* "Hack your enemies to meaty bits" *(Postal 2,* expansion pack); "More fun than shooting your neighbor's cat" *(Point Blank);* "Escape. Dismember. Massacre" *(Die by the Sword);* "Kill your friends guilt-free" *(Guilty*

Dylan Klebold and Eric Harris (above) made this videotape of themselves practicing with the very same weapons they would use to murder twelve students and one teacher. Game developers of *Postal 2: Share the Pain* apparently modeled the appearance of that game's "shooter" (the player that a gamer controls) after Klebold and Harris (see below).

Moreover, dialogue in *Postal 2* refers jokingly to the violent electronic game *Doom*, which Harris referred to in another videotape as a perfect depiction of the carnage they were planning. (Photos by Richard Abanes, taken from video of Harris and Klebold in accord with the Colorado Open Records Act; screen shot of *Postal 2* courtesy of Running With Scissors, taken by Richard Abanes during game play.)

Gear); "As easy as killing babies with axes" *(Carmageddon);* "Get in touch with your gun-toting, testosterone-pumping, cold-blooded murdering side" *(Doom).* There is no end to such marketing snippets, game-play highlights, and reviews.

Moreover, this exaltation of violence in games is sometimes merged with reality in ways that make it all the more impactful. *Mercenaries: Playground of Destruction,* for example, uses real-world news-footage clips to open the game while simultaneously running newscast-like voice-overs that set the scenario. The game focuses on military forces in North Korea that have staged a violent coup, resulting in caches of nuclear weapons that are close to being obtained by "known terrorist elements." In response, the United States sends in peacekeeping troops and issues a "Deck of 52" wanted men and women, similar to the U.S.–issued cards of wanted Iraqi military and political personages. Game players are mercenaries sent in to help out: "No Limits, No Rules, No Mercy."[18]

And then there is *F.E.A.R.: First Encounter Assault and Recon,* which is one of the most stunningly realistic FPS games to date. Although hardly realistic in its supernatural storyline, it is "being modeled after an over-the-top action movie" and is "unflinchingly violent."[19] Its realism extends to making battles as true to life as possible, duplicating with high accuracy the kinds of things a real soldier would feel, see, and hear in the real world:

> The gun battles are extremely dramatic. Bullets that barely miss you kick up showers of sparks along metal railings and tear holes in walls, while grenades and other explosive weapons send out concussive shock waves that shake your screen and leave your character's ears ring-

ing afterward. It's natural for first-person shooters to be suspenseful....It's another thing entirely to watch your teammates get blasted to bits, see their blood spattered on walls, and watch as blood pours from a punctured artery or a severed head. And...you're showered by sparks and glass shards while some guy is leaping at your face, boot first.[20]

F.E.A.R. is without doubt a phenomenal game—but not for children. The game *Manhunt* is also fascinating and intricately crafted. Once more, however, it is not for children. It is so horrifically bloody that even favorable reviewers have mentioned its violence:

> One of the problems with *Manhunt* is that shooter sequences get really overbearing toward the end. You're just gunning down so many people; blowing so many people's heads off that you'll just grow numb to all the violence after a while....Admittedly, the highlight of *Manhunt* is its graphic violence. Each of the numerous weapons in the game can be used to execute victims in one of three distinctly different ways, each one usually more brutal than the last. And these sequences are very, very graphic. They're very M-rated. [21]

"M" Means "M"

There are four basic genres of video games that normally receive an M rating (some games within them, however, are rated "T"). Each one presents a diverse set of enemies that must be taken down:

- *Occult-Paranormal,* such as *BloodRayne 2, Stubbs the Zombie, Cold Fear, Silent Hill 3,* and *Blood 2.* Enemies are usually the undead, demons, humans, or any combination of them. The games are often ultragory in depicting explicit carnage (for example, someone's brains being eaten by zombies, or vampires sucking blood).

- *Fantasy-SciFi,* such as *Halo, Alien vs. Predator, Oni, No One Lives Forever, Deus Ex,* and *XIII.* Enemies are aliens, monsters, mythological creatures, or humans. Although violent, these games often possess a cartoonlike feel.

- *Realistic Crime,* such as *Grand Theft Auto, 25 to Life, The Punisher, Manhunt,* and *Pirates of the XXI Century.* Enemies are other humans (drug lords, street thugs, ghetto gangs, innocent bystanders). Such games are so realistic that in some places they look like movies.

- *Realistic Military,* such as *Battlefield 2, Men of Valor, Call of Duty, Soldier of Fortune, Ghost Recon, Splinter Cell, Cold Winter,* and *Metal Gear Solid.* Enemies are other humans (soldiers, mercenaries, guards, spies). These are perhaps the most realistic of all video games, especially those that are designed by the U.S. military (for example, *America's Army* and *Close Combat: First to Fight*).

The Kid Connection

Not surprisingly, game makers are continuing to make violent games at a breakneck pace, including some deliberately designed to appeal to younger players. Some developers are luring young kids to their products by removing the more explicit content of M-rated games like *Duke Nukem*, formatting those versions for handheld Game Boy units, then marketing such games to children as young as five years old.[22]

The goal is to create "brand loyalty" in kids so they will purchase companion products with the same name later. "Duke," in other

The advertisement for this shooter game shows just how far some game developers are willing to go to desensitize children to violence and its effects. Here we see cute little characters, some of whom already have half of their heads blown off, running around in fear of you (the shooter).

Your job is to clear the planet of the cute little creatures (the invaders), which in reality are sadistic and racist monsters. (Note the heart-shaped balloons that are reminiscent of either Care Bears cartoons or just simply childhood. Other scenes include blood spattering against a backdrop of lollipop trees and rainbows.)

Even secular reviewers have described this game as a blend of "sick, dark humor" wherein "blood sprays in every direction." (Screen shots courtesy of Majesco Games.)

words, is being marketed as a recognizable action figure to young players of Game Boy. But when they are old enough to buy the M-rated Duke, here is what they have to look forward to:

> The story revolves loosely around a "Mars needs women" theme, involving aliens and their abduction of scantily-clad women. As Duke, you explore everything from an alien mothership to metropolitan underbellies, including smut shops, skin flicks, strip bars....Duke allows you to be an action hero to the tenth power. If it moves, shoot it. If it doesn't move, shoot it. Anything and everything can be destroyed....You slay your way through each scenario, filling aliens full of lead, even shooting wounded adversaries as they bleed on the ground, whimpering for mercy. And all the while, Duke punctuates the violence with the type of flippantly cool asides required of our modern-day action heroes."[23]

Obviously, video-game violence is only half the problem when it comes to kids. M-rated titles usually depict women as nothing more than sex objects. We'll look further at this issue, as well as the connection between sexuality and violence, in the following chapter.

4
Mature Means Mature,
Part Two

> The current trend of turning heroines into shallow objects of sexual desire is neither needed nor warranted....This is a great opportunity to enable games to be recognized as storytelling masterpieces on par with film and stage. Game developers need to stop degrading impeccably crafted works with gratuitous sexuality.
>
> LETTER TO THE EDITOR
> *GamePro* magazine, November 2005

Overt sexuality is standard for most M-rated games, along with partial nudity and in some cases full nudity. Some very questionable images that portray women as objects have also become commonplace even in games that otherwise might be appropriate for children (that is to say, T- and E-rated games).

Sex Still Sells

Sex and sensuality (more specifically, the exploitation of women as sex objects) is a significant part of the "mature" gaming experience. This is undoubtedly because most gamers are men and boys. Male video-game creators and producers have excelled in saturating video games (including many rated T and E) with images that range from mildly offensive to nearly pornographic. Gamers encounter incessant portrayals of women as scantily clad and unrealistically well-endowed females whose curves are outrageously accentuated.

To make matters worse, these images are sometimes coupled with violence. This certainly has the potential for negatively

Advent Shadow (above) is only one of hundreds of video and computer games that depict women as perfect beauties with whom real girls and women could never even hope to compete. By the time a teenage boy reaches dating age, he has spent countless hours playing electronic games featuring women with not only extraordinarily long and slender legs, but also greatly augmented breasts in disproportion to the torso, which is itself invariably thin and muscular—for all intents and purposes, without any flaws.

The above screen shots are typical of computer and video games, except for the fact that this particular female adventure hero happens to actually be clothed. Dozens of games, however, commonly depict female characters wearing hardly any clothing. (Screen shots courtesy of Majesco Games.)

affecting youth. The National Organization for Women (NOW) has released a fact sheet citing studies that show negative effects of electronic game violence along with sexuality on young players.[1] In an official statement, the California chapter of NOW declared that the organization "strongly urges consumers to stay away from choosing violent video games for children. We believe the cruelty, degradation and sexualized violence in these games are of extreme concern for women and our rights to safety, health and equal opportunity."[2]

Again, it must be noted that even a large number of the more generic T-rated and E-rated games contain what might be

BloodRayne 2, which revolves around the adventures of a female vampire, is one of those rare video/computer games that combine extreme violence (top left) with provocatively-dressed females (top right) and occult-based sexuality as well as nudity (not shown). It is an extremely violent and sexualized game. (Screen shots courtesy of Majesco Games.)

termed as either unhealthy or offensive depictions of sexuality and sensuality. In an M-rated game such depictions might go as far as a virtually nude female vampire (invariably quite voluptuous) who strikes highly provocative poses. In a more cartoonlike T-rated game, however, the offensive image might be of a female character with breasts so large and legs so long that it would forever taint a young boy's impression of what a normal woman's body should be (not to mention how such images might help send young girls down the path of anorexia and bulimia).

Even some gamers, especially women, find such depictions of females—not only their appearance, but also the story lines surrounding them—to be degrading. In a letter to *GamePro* magazine, female gamer Jhanidya Bermeo complained that some of the magazine's advertisements were "extremely degrading and disgusting to women" and that the message being sent was that "women are worthless individuals unless they have big boobs and a butt."[3] A male gamer likewise sounded off:

> I can't help but be put off by the misuse of women in video games: In almost every game, female characters look like they belong in fashion magazines and adult films, and not in a war zone or an adventure/combat setting. Most of them wear miniskirts, tiny shorts, or microscopic bikinis; have long, gorgeous hair; and sport super-model physiques....Almost every woman in a video game looks like they're dressed for the beach or a hot night out.[4]

To their credit, *GamePro* editors responded sympathetically: "The maturing of the gameplaying audience will cause game designers to think more deeply about images and roles women play in their games."[5]

More Violence

The main concern about video games, however, continues to be the violence found in numerous M-rated titles. Gang counselors, for instance, are troubled about the various crimes that are glamorized in games like *Grand Theft Auto*. They feel that "the game not only celebrates the gang lifestyle at a time when gang membership is rising nationwide, but makes a mockery of a tragedy that's all too real."[6] Such games might not only desensitize non-gang members to violence, but also validate the gang lifestyle for "gang members and wannabes." Gang counselor José Perez complains, "For those of us out here struggling to prevent gang violence it's frustrating to see the media glorify it."[7]

Other youth workers such as Stephen Cliff (who works with youths in upstate New York) and Lisa Taylor-Austin (a "gangologist" in Connecticut) agree. Cliff explains, "Kids are culturally inoculated by other kids. So then they see this game selling in the store, about gang life, they see it as vindication." And Taylor-Austin reveals, "The kids I deal with, they don't talk about *Grand Theft Auto* like it's a game. They talk about how realistic it is."[8]

And though it seems things could not get worse, companies are now producing game controllers that look like weapons. These gaming add-ons immerse the player even more deeply into each act of violence. Game participants no longer have to control their characters with just a game pad, a mouse, or a trackball. They now can actually use a "PistolMouse," which is a realistically molded handgun complete with a rubber grip. Or for players wanting to add even more gore to their virtual murders, there is the blood-spattered "*Resident Evil 4* Chainsaw Controller" for Nintendo's GameCube.[9] It "comes with a built-in sound chip, imitating the roar of the powerful weapon....When not chopping zombies into pieces...[it] can rest on its display stand."[10]

Little Manchurian Candidates

Oddly, one of the most successful producers of violent games (that is to say, realistic First-Person Shooters) is none other than the U.S. government. Several games now being played by children and teens are identical to the type of training games being used by the military. The nation's armed forces have not only come out with their own games, but they also seem to know exactly what is happening to children and are seeking to exploit it in an effort to create better soldiers.

These training games not only familiarize troops with combat tactics, weapons, and warfare strategy, but also help desensitize them to blood, gore, death, and killing. They additionally can serve to heighten one's marksmanship, increase eye–hand coordination, quicken reflexes, and help train soldiers to make field decisions based on enemy-engagement scenarios they play out in the virtual environment.

Like adults, children and teens who play violent games do, to some degree, become "desensitized to violence, have increased levels of aggressive thoughts and behavior, and act hostile toward others."[11] And yet, the U.S. military has helped develop several commercially available First-Person Shooter games—most notably *America's Army* and *Close Combat: First to Fight*. Both games are very realistic and ultraviolent.

These games skillfully blend tactical and marksmanship elements into a variety of scenarios or "missions." *America's Army* is distributed *for free* by the U.S. Army and can be played by anyone regardless of age (since it is obtained via online download). *Close Combat: First to Fight*, however, must be purchased. But its commercial developers were helped by the U.S. Marine Corps, which uses the game as a "training aid."

In reference to *America's Army*, one online game reviewer noted humorously, but also insightfully, that it was "the first game to provide job training!"[12] Indeed, the origin of the army's game, as it turns out, can be traced to the military's desire to find recruits. It all started with a *non*-government game called *Counter-Strike*, which attracted millions of young fans, specifically teenage boys:

> For years, Army recruiters had diligently pursued the very same demographic—middle-class teenage males— with dwindling success. In late 1999, after missing their recruiting goals that year, Army officials got together with the civilian directors of a Navy think tank at the Naval Postgraduate School in Monterey to discuss ways of luring computer gamers into the military. Combat gamers not only happened to target the right age for the Army's purposes but, more importantly, possessed exactly the kind of information-processing skills the Army needed: the ability to think quickly under fire. "Our military information tends to arrive in a flood,"… said Col. Casey Wardynski, a military economist who came up with the idea for an official Army computer

game. "How do you filter that? What are your tools? What is your facility in doing that? What is your level of comfort? How much load can you bear? Kids who are comfortable with that are going to be real comfortable [with the Army]." ...

The Army/Navy team began developing a game that hopefully would turn some of its players into real soldiers....An experimental psychologist from the Navy helped tweak the game's sound effects to produce heightened blood pressure, body temperature and heart rate. It was released in digital double surround sound, which few games are. In terms of game play, it was designed as a "tactical" shooter, slower-paced, more deliberate, but with *Counter-Strike*'s demanding squad tactics and communications—a "serious" game for kids who took their war-gaming seriously. After two years of development, *America's Army* was released to the public on the first Fourth of July after 9/11....[And] it was free [via online download only]....That, too, was a calculation—one the Army hoped would weed out people who didn't know much about computers. In the wake of 9/11, the public and media reaction was, in the Army's words, "overwhelmingly positive."[13]

In other words, *America's Army* is a recruitment and public-relations tool. And although the game is free, the hitch is that the Army records all of a person's game play in a U.S. computer database—kill statistics, online playing time, the maps on which a certain gamer plays best. This is the information America's *real* army wanted, and it was willing to spend more than $8 million developing a free game to get it.[14]

A Vocational Tool

But why would the army care about tracking player proficiency, especially of the 3.3 million users who logged 60 million hours of play between July 2002 and December 2004?[15] Because such information, after being gathered for years, could help predict the soldier potential of a new recruit. The game basically reflects "the Armed Services Vocational Aptitude Battery," which assists the Army in placing someone who enlists.[16]

The *America's Army* official Web site plainly verifies this assertion (albeit inconspicuously). The game's "Frequently Asked Questions" page says that players who request information about the army "may have their gaming records matched to their real-world identities for the purpose of facilitating career placement within the Army."[17] It continues,

> Data collected within the game such as which roles and missions players spent the most time playing could be used to highlight Army career fields that map into these interest areas so as to provide the best possible match between the attributes and interests of potential Soldiers and the attributes of career fields and training opportunities.[18]

Michael Zyda, a co-developer of the game has admitted it was cleared by a senior psychologist from the Army Research Institute of Behavioral Science. Zyda has further revealed, "With respect to recruitment, actual results won't be known for four or five years, when the current raft of 13- and 14-year-olds will be old enough to join."[19]

Close Combat: First to Fight similarly reflects real military standards. It is "based on a training tool developed for the United

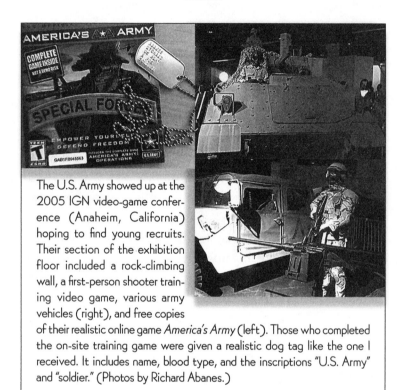

The U.S. Army showed up at the 2005 IGN video-game conference (Anaheim, California) hoping to find young recruits. Their section of the exhibition floor included a rock-climbing wall, a first-person shooter training video game, various army vehicles (right), and free copies of their realistic online game *America's Army* (left). Those who completed the on-site training game were given a realistic dog tag like the one I received. It includes name, blood type, and the inscriptions "U.S. Army" and "soldier." (Photos by Richard Abanes.)

States Marines." This "game" is billed as one in which a player can go through "the real-life combat experiences of the proud few."[20] It offers in-close tactical operations that more closely resemble special-ops maneuvers. And by no coincidence, the setting of *Close Combat* is the Middle East, in an urban warfare setting very much like Iraq.

The Plot Thickens

Both *America's Army* and *Close Combat* are unlike other shooter games in one very significant way—they do not allow players to kill for the other side. A gamer can play with only one identity—that of an American soldier. This is a radical departure from normal gaming, in which a player can be whoever or whatever they want to be: good, bad, an alien, a gangster, a wizard, a police officer, or a foreign soldier.

A few more bits of information are relevant. First, the military recently distributed an update to *America's Army* titled "Special Forces." A random decision? Hardly. A booklet produced by the Navy explains exactly why "Special Forces" was released:

> Specifically, the Department of Defense wants to double the number of Special Forces soldiers, so essential did they prove in Afghanistan and northern Iraq; consequently, orders have trickled down the chain of command and found application in the current release of *America's Army*, which features Special Forces roles, missions, and equipment.[21]

Second, a 2004 issue of *National Defense Magazine* boldly proclaimed, "At least half a million video-game aficionados each month play what has become a successful military recruiting tool: *America's Army*." This article also noted that an upcoming version "will also be the first to feature a real-life combat scenario. Players will step into the shoes of a 26-member special force A-team that used Javelin missiles to repel an Iraqi motorized rifle company backed by artillery, tanks and armored personnel carriers."[22]

Third, the military knows that other FPS games are drawing the kind of players they want. So, at numerous Web sites, whenever someone chooses to watch game trailers, clip scenes, or game-play movies, they must first watch an advertisement for the U.S. Army. And these advertisements precede footage from some of the most violent of all FPS games (for example, *The Punisher* and *25 Years to Life*—see pages 59–61).[23]

All of this back-and-forth play between the military and the entertainment industry began in earnest with the 1999 founding of the Institute for Creative Technologies (ICT), a center within the University of Southern California (USC) school system. "ICT is a $45 million joint Army/USC venture" that was "designed to link up the military with academia and the entertainment and video game industries."[24] ICT has been involved with

- Paramount Pictures in training soldiers to deal with crisis situations

- entertainment executives from whom support has been drawn to develop soldiers using "software applications"

- Hollywood personnel, who have been tapped to create "futuristic weapons, vehicles, equipment and uniforms for the Army."[25]

The military, using ICT as a go-between, is looking to Hollywood for the perfect future soldier, who is now being called the Objective Force Warrior (OFW). In other words, Hollywood is dreaming up the warrior and the military is trying to make those dreams a reality. Hollywood also is helping out in other ways. For example, "'America's Army' features sound effects by moviemaker George Lucas' company, SkyWalker....Sound effects from the movie 'Terminator II' were provided at no charge."[26]

ICT also came out with yet another popular warfare game that is linked directly to the military: *Full Spectrum Warrior* (Xbox). This game was a result of ICT pursuing its goal of creating "immersive, interactive, real-time training simulations to help the Army teach decision making and leadership skills" in cooperation "with the U.S. Army Research, Development and Engineering Command, Simulation, Training and Instrumentation (RDE COM STRI), Training and Doctrine Command (TRADOC)."[27] And children, simply put, are being used as guinea pigs.

Video Games and the Military—Industrial Complex

Xbox's manufacturer (Microsoft) is the producer of yet another first person shooter, *Halo 2*, which sports as its main character a U.S. soldier who wears gear reminiscent of ICT's Objective Force Warrior (see above). These games are preparing children to be the soldiers of both the near *and* distant future. Moreover, ICT recently struck a deal with the CIA to provide games that will help analysts "think outside the box" with regard to terrorists.[28]

Other games produced in cooperation with, or association with, the military include *SOCOM II* (U.S. Naval Special Warfare Command) and *Kuma War* (Department of Defense). Further, as of December 2004, a simulation center had been set up at the Institute for Defense Analysis, "which is charged with adapting off-the-shelf games for use in the Defense Department."[29]

In January 2005, the air force released the game *USAF: Air Dominance*, which was scheduled to be taken around to

"NASCAR races and other events" in hopes of finding teens who, after enjoying the game, will sign up for the service.[30] Critical Mass Interactive, the game's developer, said that the air force game came into being after the company "got a document on one page that said, 'you have three months to get it done.'"[31]

In a word, computer and video games have become nothing less than a prime recruitment and public-relations tool for the U.S. military, as evidenced by dozens of recent articles in *National Defense Magazine*.[32] One of these declared, "Computer games—which entertain millions of U.S. teenagers—are beginning to breathe fresh life into military recruiting and training." Michael Macedonia—senior scientist for the U.S. Army Simulation, Training, and Instrumentation Command (STRICOM)—made it very plain: "We win wars with these games, because they help train soldiers."[33]

The "gaming" strategy has apparently worked for the military. Consider, for instance, the story of Alexandre Perni, a player who was quoted in *Electronic Gaming Monthly* magazine in September 2005:

> I bought *Full Spectrum Warrior* a while ago and loved it. I also found out it was a training tool used for the US Army. I was out of high school and was looking for a job, so after beating *FSW*, I visited a recruiter for the United States Marine Corps. I enrolled, training to become an infantryman. I'm now in camp, getting ready to pass the Crucible. Most people I talk to think I'm an idiot for joining the USMC—and I am—but I'm more of an idiot for joining because of playing FSW.[34]

Not surprisingly, it was announced in late 2004 that the military had licensed *America's Army* (formerly just a computer-based game) to the commercial entertainment company Ubisoft "in an effort to reach millions of youngsters who play Microsoft X-Box and Sony Playstation console games."[35] Kids will eventually be able to play *America's Army* on even their cell phones! This puts a very twenty-first-century spin on the old military recruiter's motto: "UNCLE SAM WANTS YOU."

Electronic games are not going to go away, especially now that the government has gotten involved in both the manufacturing and distribution of video games for their own purposes. Video games are here to stay, and kids will be playing them. What are parents, educators, and youth workers going to do about it? How can children and teens be protected?

These are the important questions. But before making any decisions, a commitment must be made to meet the challenge calmly—and a few things must be remembered. Our next chapter will explore some aspects of whether or not a person should play video games.

5
To Play or Not to Play?

It's legitimately difficult for someone
who wasn't raised playing video games
to understand their true impact on our emotions,
our values, our choices, our lives.

JENNIFER TSAO
managing editor, *Electronic Gaming Monthly*

‹

There are all kinds of video games: good, bad, and ugly. And at the extreme end of the latter category there are those games that are especially tasteless and, it would be argued, devoid of any value (for example, the senselessly violent *Postal* series, the inane *Big Mutha Truckers*, and *Playboy Mansion*). Many other video games, however, despite having mature edges, are works of brilliant artistry.

Video games cannot be isolated from other forms of artistic expression that are widely accepted and respected. All use mature themes, including murder, adultery, fornication, suicide, and nudity (for example, operas, masterful paintings and sculptures, classic novels, and award-winning films). It is not necessarily the themes or scenes that determine whether or not a video game is good or bad, but rather, *how* such themes or scenes are depicted and *what* overall message is being delivered through them. What is the context of the game's mature aspects?

A good non-video-game example might be The Lord of the Rings trilogy of movies. There are some truly disturbing scenes in these films, which show not only violence, but violence combined with some very nasty—perhaps even demonic—creatures. (They're reminiscent of something you might run into while playing *Doom 3* and trying to make your way back to Marine headquarters from deep inside some research facility on Mars.) But what messages are being communicated via Tolkien's work? What messages are being communicated through *Doom 3*? These are the important questions to ask.

The Lord of the Rings consistently exalts the good characters and their steadfast commitment to defeating evil, no matter how terrifying it may be or how overwhelming the odds are against good. (An exception perhaps is Borimir, who at least saw the error of his ways and repented before dying.) The horrific nature and looks of the dreaded Orcs heighten the sense of evil pervading Tolkien's world and residing in the dark forces seeking to take over all of Middle Earth. The imagery fits the story line and is necessary.

But what about games and movies like *Doom,* "the most successful first-person shooter franchise in video games"?[1] It is true that this series contains occult symbolism and imagery, but the all-important question again is this: What messages are being communicated? Without spoiling the game's story line, suffice it to say that the enemies you must defeat are either the undead (former humans whose evil side has been heightened to the point of their mutation into hideous monsters) or demonic entities. The occult symbolism is not glamorized or exalted. Occult pentagrams and satanic-like rituals are associated throughout the game with supremely *negative* moments in the game when you must use all of your skills and game experience to get out of danger—defeat the evil.

Bringing Out the Good

The Lord of the Rings brings to the front of my mind a plethora of themes that could launch nearly any Bible study—love, honor, commitment, loyalty, faithfulness, repentance, forgiveness, trust, bravery, and self-sacrifice. I have found these same themes reaching out to me over and over again while immersed in games like *Doom 3* and many other games such as *Halo; Battlefield 2;* and *Brothers in Arms: Earned in Blood.*

Call of Duty 2, for example, somehow manages to submerge you deep beneath the waves of sheer terror that must wash over any soldier who finds himself in the midst of an all-out battle for his life. While playing the game I often found myself completely forgetting that my buddies to the left of me were not real. It was *my* responsibility to provide suppressing fire for them as they moved forward. What if I ran out of ammo? What if I didn't shoot where the enemy was positioned? Was there a sniper who was going to take out the first guy to pop his head up?

A similar feeling—not to mention a massive dose of adrenaline—always overcomes me when I play *Battlefield 2*. Unlike *Call of Duty 2*, though, which takes place during World War II, *Battlefield 2* captures the experiences of modern warfare—usually set in the Middle East (just like in the real world). There's nothing quite like being a medic in the midst of relentless enemy fire, but knowing you have only 15 seconds to get to a fellow soldier who's been fragged. He's a dead man if you don't help. What do you do, especially when you can hear him crying out, "Medic!" Do you run? Hide? Do you wait until the last moment, hoping that you can save your buddy in the second or two it takes your enemy to reload? Such games increase a person's ability to work with others, strategize, think quickly under pressure, and actually form bonds.

And war-based games are able to create some of the most emotionally riveting experiences players can have (see sidebar). As Vince Zampella, chief creative officer for *Call of Duty 2*, has described it: "That intensity of war. The feeling of 'Oh my god, this is real. People actually went through this.' The emotion, the intensity—that's what we're capturing." He adds, "We're creating a world that's all around you. It's not just like, there's three guys in front of you; there's a war going on all around you."[2]

Putting Things in Perspective

Yes, many video games are rated "M." And yes, it is also true that some of these games contain not only graphic violence but also occult allusions (for example, *Doom 3*). But so do some of the greatest books, films, and theatrical productions of the last hundred years. It's crucial to note, despite the sensationalistic coverage of video games in the media, that M-rated games represent only a fraction of the games produced and sold. Consider these facts about video-game ratings and content in 2004 and 2005:

- Among games produced, 54 percent were rated "E," 33 percent were rated "T," and 12 percent were rated "M." (With movies, 55 percent are released with an R-rating.)
- Bestselling games are consistently those rated "T" or lower.
- In October 2005, four out of the top-ten-selling games were sports-related (soccer, football, hockey, and golf), two were driving games, three were cartoon action games, and only one could be called violent—*Rainbow Six: Lockdown,* a military-based shooter.[3]

Consider, though, the level of criticism on games in light of the many TV programs and movies that regularly show real-world violence (for example, *The Shield*). Further, sports fans enjoy brutality each weeknight in a myriad of WWF wrestling matches and NHL hockey games. And then there is always *Ultimate Fight Challenge* (mixed martial-arts fighting on Spike TV), during which fans cheer caged combatants trying to either pummel each other into unconsciousness or choke their opponent until they pass out (or subject them to my favorite, the dreaded "arm-bar," which always forces an opponent to give up or have their arm broken in two).

As for concerns about sexuality in games, we have TV

commercials (think Budweiser, assorted automobiles, and even Burger King) that regularly display a bevy of silicone-enhanced "babes" clad in skimpy shorts, bikinis, or tight dresses—during prime-time kiddie hours. Don't forget, either, the MTV music videos and specials that show gyrating women in bikinis and serve up nonstop sexual innuendo—all watched by children and young teens.

And, of course, children under 17 years old can get into R-rated movies, which are allowed to contain full frontal nudity and seriously steamy sex scenes. In an opinion letter to *PC Gamer*, one avid player commented on this: "You're supposed to be 17 years or older to play [*Grand Theft Auto* and other M-rated games]. Well, to get into an R-rated movie, you have to be 17 as well. No one is angry about nudity/sex scenes in movies."[4]

Indeed, R-rated movies usually contain much more graphic violence and sexuality than anything found in a video game (not to mention the kind of adult material accessed by children and teens on HBO, Cinemax, and assorted pay-per-view channels). But few people these days, including politicians, are voicing concerns and criticisms that might offend the powers in Hollywood.

The frustration and even anger on the part of people who are trying to protect children is understandable. But the route to a solution is *not*

- to scapegoat video games because the battle against smut and violence on TV and cable seems all but lost

- or worse yet, to make political hay out of attacking what seems currently to be an easy target

And think about this: Many of the explicit sexual scenes and nudity commonly found on TV and cable (and often watched by children or teens) would most certainly earn an Adults Only rating from the ESRB (Entertainment Software Ratings Board) if the material were to appear in a video game. At the very least, such images would earn the Mature label for a game.

We need go no further than the highly popular and influential MTV and MTV2 networks to see the kind of real-world images to which I am referring. In fact, a February 2005 Associated Press article titled "Study: MTV Delivers a Diet of 'Sleaze'" covered a recently released Parents Television Council study. The study revealed that the programming of the youth-driven MTV network is apparently far worse than the content aired on major networks: "During one week last March, the watchdog Parents Television Council said it counted 3,056 flashes of nudity or sexual situations and 2,881 verbal references to sex." This is significant because MTV's main viewers are as young as 12 years old—a full five years younger than the age recommendation for an M-rated video game!

So if there is any solution that could usefully be implemented, it might be to not focus on video games as the problem, but instead hold TV networks and producers of movies, music CDs, and DVDs to the very same rating system and restrictions now placed on the games. This would result in a more evenhanded approach toward all of the industries and lessen the unbalanced criticism of video games. Then, as Jennifer Tsao, managing editor of *Electronic Gaming Monthly,* pointed out, "Anyone complaining about GTA's [*Grand Theft Auto's*] sex and violence would have to put the game up against films or TV with the same rating."[5]

The Effects of Violence

What about the gamers who have committed crimes in apparent response to the video games they were playing? It is true there have been some links between a few gamers and some truly horrifying crimes (see page 12). But as Steven Johnson, author of *Everything Bad Is Good for You*, has insightfully noted, "Psychopathic people are always influenced by the media around them—Manson by the Beatles, John Hinckley by *Taxi Driver*. You can't point to an isolated incident and condemn the whole media."[6]

It's much more important to look at the broad picture. Although video-game production and sales have steadily risen since 1996, violent crime in America's general population has remained about the same.[7] Even more relevant is the fact that U.S. Department of Justice statistics from 1993/94 to 2003/04 show a *decline* of violence among youth—ages 12 and over. (This period saw the release of games such as the Grand Theft Auto series and the advent of Playstation 2 and Xbox.) Likewise, homicide rates among youth and young adults—ages 14 to 17 and 18 to 24—dropped from 1993 to 2002 (statistics from 2003/04 unavailable).[8]

Clearly, video games have not been creating a whole generation of cold-blooded killers. On the other hand, however, some studies indicate that the violence in certain video games can affect some children negatively by making them more prone to aggression, usually for limited periods of time. But of course, exposure to violent media of any kind causes these same effects. Moreover, it must be remembered that many factors determine whether a child will become agitated in response to media violence.

So this is not necessarily an issue of whether or not video

games are inherently more dangerous than other media forms. It is more related to the effects of media violence in general on kids. And those effects, when compared to other factors, do not seem to be major. According to U.S. Surgeon General David Satcher, the various forms of violent media (including video games) fall into the "Small Effect Size" category of influence. There are as many as 27 other risk factors that rate "higher than exposure to violent media—like socioeconomic status, academic failure, and poor parent-child relationships....The single biggest factor was simply being male."[9]

A Wrap-Up of Concerns

In addition to violence, there also exist other areas of caution about video games that must be noted: excessive sexuality, ethical and moral relativism, stereotyping of women (and ethnic groups), religious imagery that might be offensive to some, and use of profanity. Some game developers, as one gamer has rightly noted, "are reaching into some very dark places and they are desensitizing gamers to extreme cruelty, sexism, and violence."[10]

There is also a tendency in some games to glamorize criminal (and usually dangerous) behavior. The game *Need for Speed: Most Wanted,* for instance, is based entirely on illegal racing on city streets—a very big problem in California: "The more races you win and the better you can evade the fuzz, the higher you climb on the 'blacklist,' which opens up new events and goods."[11]

And what about the often over-the-top sexuality? It must be stated here that, when it comes to *explicit* or *graphic* sexuality, those kinds of games are few and far between (for example, *Playboy: The Mansion; Leisure Suit Larry,* and *Grand Theft Auto*—the modded original version—to name several).[12] All of these, too, it must be remembered, are rated Adults Only. However, it should also be said that sexploitation of women in games is so common that one magazine offers a *Girls of Gaming* collection that is actually devoted to the hypersexualized images of female video characters. An advertisement reads, "Filled with nearly two hundred images of gaming's hottest and baddest babes, the bundle pack for *Play* magazine's annual *Girls of Gaming* is the ultimate collection of video game babe imagery."[13]

Clearly, some aspects of the video-game industry need to grow up. Profanity and rough language also remain a problem. Some producers argue that this adds a level of realism to the game (for example, the shooter *F.E.A.R.*). But not all gamers agree such "realism" is necessary. In a letter to *PC Gamer*, one player asked, "Why can't publishers record a curse-free localized sound option…?" The hard-core gaming magazine responded in a way that might surprise many people: "We're in total agreement with you on your suggestion….Publishers are losing customers to this issue when there's a very quick fix."[14]

A word must also be said about the spirituality that is often presented in video games. It is usually occult-based—or at the very least, occult-laced. This could be a serious problem for Christian parents, whose faith stands adamantly against such forms of religious expression. The spirituality in games must be taken into consideration by parents seeking appropriate material for their children. After all, game makers, like all other artists share their opinions and beliefs through the art they create. Consequently, some games will advance certain religious ideas, concepts, or views that conflict with a family's expressed faith. Most of the time, however, games use religious allusions simply because of their powerful symbolism and emotional appeal. As we've emphasized, the context of the material is crucial.

Another problem associated with video games is the level of time commitment they require, which might distract young people (and even adults) from more important matters. Related to this, a few games have rather steep learning curves, which could prove frustrating for children and teens not intellectually advanced enough to handle a complex game.

Finally, it must also be noted that some people become addicted to video games, getting so fixated that playing begins affecting them in negative ways—not only psychologically, but also physically. A case in point would be the national obsession with games in Korea, where 35 percent of the population (totaling 17 million) plays. Many gamers commonly play for hours—sometimes for days—with no real breaks. There is an actual epidemic of game addiction in Korea, with nearly 10,000 cases reported in 2005. This obsession caused at least two deaths from heart failure—one man died after a 50-hour marathon, while the other died after playing for 86 hours!

Lastly, also touching on the issue of time commitment, children and teens must be cautioned about the risks involved in trying to make a career out of gaming. First, it is a very competitive field that requires not only raw talent, but also the self-discipline to practice as hard as any professional athlete. Second, according to Dennis Fong (the world's first pro gamer), "Years spent honing skills in one game could literally become worthless overnight if it is decided by sponsors or by the leagues that the game is no longer popular."[15]

Accentuate the Positive

Like the many other forms of entertainment available to consumers these days, video games have both good and bad aspects. Often, not enough time is spent balancing out the problems and warnings, so the next few pages will focus on the benefits and positive side of video games.

Career Gaming

Diverse career choices are now open to members of the younger generation who know their games. The video-game industry is quickly becoming a field of study for future development of artists, computer programmers, writers, and many other talents.

As of late 2005, in fact, more than 100 colleges and universities in America were offering courses, degrees, or both associated with video games. According to the Fall 2005 *Game Career Guide*, on the list are several prestigious institutions, including Southern Methodist University, Michigan State University, and the University of California. Moreover, as of 2004, the annual salaries for a variety of positions within game-developing were more than competitive:

- *Game Design/Designer:* less than 3 years job experience ($44,000); 3 to 6 years ($52,000); more than 6 years ($67,000)

- *Art & Animation/Animator:* less than 3 years job experience ($44,800); 3 to 6 years ($65,600); more than 6 years ($73,000)

- *Programming/Technical Director:* less than 3 years job experience ($63,700); 3 to 6 years ($81,100); more than 6 years ($115,000)

- *Production/Executive Producer:* less than 3 years job experience ($52,500); 3 to 6 years ($60,800); more than 6 years ($118,400)[16]

Given the above information, it is no surprise that a number of books have now been released to help young people find careers in the field of gaming: *Game Creation and Careers* (New Riders Games); *Break into the Game Industry* (McGraw-Hill); and *Game Art: Creation, Direction, and Careers* (Charles River Media), to name but a few.

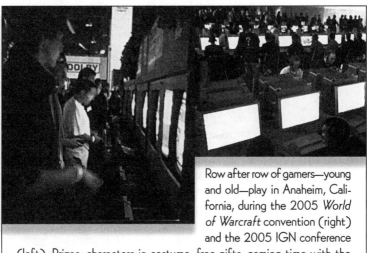

Row after row of gamers—young and old—play in Anaheim, California, during the 2005 *World of Warcraft* convention (right) and the 2005 IGN conference (left). Prizes, characters in costume, free gifts, gaming time with the hottest new titles, competitive tournaments, game-inspired artwork, and business contacts for careers in gaming made both events highly successful. (Photos by Richard Abanes.)

And as mentioned previously, video games are now a legitimate sport, wherein talented players can make a living. There even exists the Olympics-like Cyberathlete Extreme Summer Championships and Cyberathlete Extreme Winter Championships sponsored by the Cyberathlete Professional League (CPL). Prizes for these two competitions totaled $435,000 in 2005. Similarly, the World Cyber Games festival awards not only gold, silver, and bronze medals, but also large cash awards. In 2003, the games handed out $2 million to the various winners.

Medical Miracles

Some of the most beneficial uses of video games have been in the area of medicine and behavioral therapy. Recent studies suggest that patients who must endure painful medical procedures or chronic pain can find physical relief through playing. According to Dr. Bryan Raudenbush—associate professor of Psychology at Wheeling Jesuit University—the level of "pain distraction" afforded by video games is significant. The most "distracting" games were sports and fight-based games.[17] It is beyond doubt now that games "help kids tolerate pain and adapt to their surroundings more readily during hospital stays. Many progressive children's hospitals now consider game consoles part of their patient rooms' standard equipment."[18]

Children are even being allowed to play games on a Game Boy just before going into surgery as a way of relaxing them (for example, at Children's Hospital of Philadelphia). According to anesthesiologist Dr. Anu Patel of University Hospital, Newark, New Jersey, "Children are just so happy with the Game Boy that they actually do forget where they are." This surprising and wonderful benefit of video games directly led to the creation in 2001 of the California-based Get-Well Gamers Foundation, which is "dedicated to bringing electronic entertainment to children in healthcare facilities."[19]

Playing the Field

A gamer can receive major financial backing from corporate sponsors who are looking for players to represent their products. These companies include such heavyweights as MTV, Converse, Samsung, Sony, and Nokia. In fact, an organization known as the Global Gaming League helps find gamer-corporation matches by seeking out the best players from hundreds of colleges.

There are indeed careers waiting out there—and high-paying ones at that. For example, the five-man ESWC champion team took home a check for $40,000. And at the popular QuakeCon (6000 attendees), the *Doom* 3 single-player champion of 2005 won $25,000. This is just the start. A professional gamer like the celebrated Fatal1ty (Johnathan Wendel), who is a college dropout, can haul in $300,000 annually.

Video games also seem able to help children with Attention Deficit Disorder (ADD) focus their attention better for prolonged periods of time. Prescribing "play" for ADD patients, which is becoming more common, is known as *video-game therapy.* Approximately 50 clinics nationwide are now using the new S.M.A.R.T. BrainGames system, which is based on neural feedback, to help kids. Patients are actually able to transfer their game-playing concentration skills to other activities, such as schoolwork and sports.[20]

Finally, it has been documented that video games can not only increase hand–eye coordination, but also "stimulate different parts of the brain, and exercise its capacity to understand and process complex situations."[21] Further, the great deal of thought that must go into learning most games often takes a measure of strategy, mastering various controls, memorizing game maps, and sometimes even learning commerce and trading skills. Some games even rely on the use of logic, analysis, and research—all while simultaneously teaching basic computer skills and new technology.

More Pluses

In addition to the above benefits, there are several other pluses that must be noted—the most obvious being the sheer "fun factor" of video games. People, especially adults, need downtime and periods of recreation to relieve the stress of the daily grind. Games are now legitimate forms of adult recreation, along with fine dining, sports, and the theater. And they can be played by adults and children together—a sort of high-tech version of the miniature-golf family outing.

There is the whole social aspect of game-playing as well. For example, innumerable "clans" (small groups of like-minded gamers) have sprung up all over the world. These highly social, tight-knit communities that regularly play together online or at LAN—Local-Area Network—parties have almost become the cultural backbone of a whole new generation. And the rise of MMOs (see page 22) has put individuals from various countries in touch with each other as never before. Such games have created a myriad of social communities based on a common interest and on genuine care for each other.

A degree of self-expression also can be enjoyed through video games—and not just for the designers and creators. Today's most advanced games allow players to shape their onscreen character's physical appearance, attributes, clothing, talents, societal standing, and mental attributes. Entire worlds can be created and then, based on decisions made in the game, those worlds will change to reflect the player's choices.

This latter point relates to the opportunity for the discussion of ethical and moral issues given by games. In *True Crime: New York City*, for example, bad choices made by players bring bad consequences to the appearance of the player's locale. The environment changes in response to a player's choices to "let crime run rampant (or clean up the city of crooks). Businesses will open or close depending on how dangerous an area is, and the appearance of the neighborhood will either deteriorate or sparkle depending on how much crime you stop/allow."[22] A wide variety of choices must be made, which will gradually turn a character into a good police officer or a bad one. All of this ultimately leads to an end-of-game scenario that reflects how you have played. This can make for some fascinating conversations—even within families—about the world, the choices we make, and how those choices affect things.

Using Common Sense

Although there are aspects of video games about which parents should be concerned, what is needed is not rigid censorship, banning, or laws against them. The real need is for common sense to be used by the people whose responsibility it is to take care of children—parents, primarily, followed by child-care givers, educators, and members of the video-game industry. Several points are worth remembering:

1. *Video games are not inherently evil, destructive, or lacking in positive benefits.* Sports titles, problem-solving/puzzle titles, action–adventure titles, and some enjoyable role-playing games account for a very large portion of sales.[23]

2. *Players most at risk of being negatively influenced by highly violent and sexualized images in games are children and early teens.* This is why there are ratings on games. Mature adults playing mature games, although we may disagree with their entertainment choices, are exercising their freedoms. Very little research has shown that adults are as heavily influenced by video games as are children. So we must take care in the area of rigid censorship. Moreover, the research conducted so far on children and the negative effects of video games on them is not conclusive. The studies have been limited, and controls have not always been consistent.

3. *Games that are multiplayer-enabled for the Internet can help a child or teen bond with new friends, find companionship, and experience true community.* According to University of California professor Robert Nideffer, a specialist in art and computer science, "players are actively participating with other people in a very social space."[24] This is something parents should encourage. Gamers do have social lives, and through their games they develop social skills.

4. *The feeling of accomplishment that comes with mastering a game can build the self-confidence and self-esteem of a child or teen.* This holds especially true for the consumers game developers are targeting: teenage boys. Psychology professor B.J. Fogg of Stanford University explains, "Video games, better than anything else in our culture, deliver rewards to people, especially teenage boys." He adds, "Teenage boys are wired to seek competency; to master our world and get better at stuff. Video games, in dishing out rewards, can convey to people that their competency is growing, you can get better at something second by second."[25]

5. *Parents must not forget that teens and children mature at different rates.* Just as books and movies must be judged case by case, so too must video games be carefully reviewed. In other words, parents and others who work with children must be involved with determining which games will be played by the children in their care. Kids *cannot* be left alone to make decisions about their games.

6. *Finally, there is no proof that children or teens will turn violent, become sexually deviant, or become occultists simply because of a book, movie, TV program, or video game.* This final point brings up a crucial issue that must be stressed and not forgotten. Things like electronic games, movies, and other forms of entertainment do play a part in child development. Major studies, polls and surveys, and anecdotal evidence all demonstrate that many children do indeed dabble with or boldly copy the things they experience through entertainment—things associated with violence, sex, and spirituality. As far back as 1972, the U.S. Surgeon General's report plainly noted, "We know that children imitate and learn from everything

they see: parents, fellow children, school, the media."[26] Reinforcing this, in the year 2000, American Academy of Pediatrics president Donald Cook said before the U.S. Senate Commerce committee, "Children learn the ways of the world by observing and imitating—they cannot help but be influenced by media."[27]

When it comes to video games—indeed, when it comes to any form of entertainment—the bottom line is "watch, read, and listen responsibly," and play responsibly.[28] In an effort to assist parents in doing this, I offer the final chapter of this guide to video games, which will cover some of the best family-friendly games I have found to date.

6
Family-Friendly Fun

[You are] a weary traveler on the most hazardous of journeys. Mile upon mile you've ridden in search of the power to save your one true love. Yet now you find yourself here, standing in the shadow of a beast who will devastate the tiny, insignificant being who dared to disturb his slumber—unless you arm yourself with the one weapon large enough to slay him....The weapon? Your mind. And should you use it wisely, you shall topple a creature whose size is comparable only to your valor.

PRINT ADVERTISEMENT
Shadow of the Colossus

According to Journalist Chris Morris, whose "Game Over" column at CNN.com has become a must-read for video-game industry watchers, the current scrutiny of video games is a direct result of their penetration into the arena of influential entertainment forms. "It happened with cinema. It happened with music. It happened with comic books," says Morris. "Now it's happening with games." As Brady Fiechter, executive editor of *Play* magazine, noted in late 2005, "The academic discussion on games is really just beginning. We're defining the rules as we go along, as technology and experimentation continually evolve."[1]

Parents, educators, and church leaders certainly must take care with regard to the kinds of video games they endorse and allow into their homes. But at the same time they must refrain from becoming overconcerned with "video games" in general. There are a multitude of enjoyable games appropriate for the whole family. (As with all types of games, those that fall into the family-friendly category run the gamut from the delightfully cute and entertaining to the very poorly done.) The following pages give just a small sampling of some of the best games for all age ranges.

For the Little Ones

One of the cutest games to hit the market in 2005 was *Nintendogs* (available on Nintendo's DS unit). The object of the game is to raise an adorable little puppy into an obedient best friend. You accomplish this task by training your on-screen bundle of fur just as you would train any real pooch. You give your dog rewards, play with it, pet it, scold it, and give it commands—except with *Nintendogs* you must use either a stylus or a built-in microphone. You can even give your little e-friend a variety of toys to gnaw on as you watch in delight, or you can dress your puppy in various kinds of pet clothes.

Another video game primarily for younger players is *Mario Superstar Baseball*, a descendant of the classic *Super Mario Brothers* video game. In this game are included several video-game superstar characters, such as Luigi and the famous Donkey Kong. The object is fairly simple: Create two superstar teams from a variety of available characters and then—"Play ball!" You can link players together for bonus joint-skills, earn special "stars" to help you win, or engage in various "mini" games that can be accessed during regular game play.

We Love Katamari (Playstation 2) has an altogether different player goal. This game's objective is simply to roll a ball around many different environments and scenes and by so doing pick up various objects that "stick" to the ball. This may sound oversimple, to be blunt, but it is actually quite intriguing. The ball grows larger as you complete each task, which in turn enables you to pick up larger objects (even buildings). The game has a very cartoonlike feel to it, complete with bright colors and striking images that will capture the attention of both kids and adults. Though the story plot is a bit odd, it is merely a vehicle for the real fun stuff— collecting goodies by rolling around an ever-growing ball.

For children who are slightly older, *The Incredibles: Rise of the Underminer* is a great alternative. It pits cartoon heroes Frozone and Mr. Incredible against a villain in Metroville known as "The Underminer." To destroy this enemy, the two heroes use a variety of superhuman gifts. Frozone can do just about anything with his powers to manipulate cold (for example, make ice bridges). Mr. Incredible, on the other hand, relies on brute strength, which opens up a world of possibilities. The cartoon graphics are absolutely stunning—in fact, they are near movie-quality. There is a little bit of everything in this game for players of all ages (hence the E rating): fast action, stealth moves, and full-out battles between good guys and bad guys.

I Need a Hero

In the realm of games for more advanced players there exist a myriad of action-packed titles that draw heavily upon the "hero" theme. The most obvious game in this class is *City of Heroes*—an MMORPG that allows players to become a superhero whose main objective is to battle evil, either individually or in a team. As a player, your location is Paragon City. Your enemies may be one or more villains belonging to a criminal faction that infests your locale.

One of the most outstanding aspects of this game is the way a player can create a very complex appearance for his or her character. Your hero can be big, small, male, or female. He (or she) can be helmeted or masked—or not. And the assortment of superpowers at your disposal is nearly unlimited. You can battle your foes using flames, speed, energy blasts, ice, flight, teleportation, brute strength, or some other skill.

The graphics in this game are wonderful. You behold them as you leap from rooftop to rooftop, fly to some destination in need of you (with your cape trailing in the wind), or simply take a casual walk up and down the streets of Paragon City. Additional visual delights are found in the game's various environmental zones, which present different situations, people, surroundings, and potential enemies: Steel Canyon, Kings Row, Perez Park, Striga Isle, and Dark Astoria, to name but a few. You never know what might happen in these and other areas, but it is your job to make things right.

Quests propel the game, making it not only fun but also challenging, as the following description from a special *PC Gamer* article notes:

> You arrive on the island not by train or highway, but by smuggler ship....Immediately you make a mission-dispensing contact in this industrial area: a terrorized

ghetto in which the local baddies, The Council, are causing havoc. Initial quest arcs allow you to explore warehouses, tackling the smuggling that is funding their criminal operations. As the quests continue you are drawn further inland....As the missions develop, so does the sense of danger and aura of mystery....You'll discover a Sky Raider base....a huge volcano....robot sentries...[and] a supernatural cult, augmented with the darkest technologies.[2]

Another hero-based video game is *Lego Star Wars*. This fun title blends Lego-style figures with the George Lucas characters. The result is an entertaining, slightly offbeat game that is visually amusing. The Star Wars cast includes favorites such as Obi-Wan Kenobi and Anakin Skywalker, and players are treated to seeing these and other characters as little Lego Jedi Knights who wield their lightsabers as well as the heroes on the silver screen (you'll have to see the game to understand what a Lego-ized version of Chewbacca looks like).

Last but not least, the hero category includes a plethora of sports video games that allow players to become a sports celebrity. In *Madden NFL 06*, for example, you actually mold and shape yourself into a star football player by first selecting your parents. You then progress through a career with the help of various characters, including some based on real-world players. You can eventually land a great contract with a pro team and even get an agent to help you establish a big-time career in the NFL. Similar games include *NHL 06* (hockey), *MLB 06* (baseball) and *NBA Live 06* (basketball).

There are various alternative sports games as well, such as *SSX on Tour* (downhill skiing), *Nascar 06* and *Forza Motorsport* (auto racing), and any of the great *Tony Hawk* titles (skateboarding). All of these latter sports games give older kids and teens (as well as adults) thrilling and competitive action along with environmental settings far different from the basic baseball or football stadium or sports arena. *Forza Motorsport,* for instance, offers more than 200 different cars you can drive in competitions held at re-creations of real racing tracks from around the world (as well as invented courses that wind through major cities, like New York).

Christian Gaming

One of the most surprising turns of events in the video-game industry has been the introduction of new Christian games into the mainstream market. Several developers are now working on various titles that include a First-Person Shooter (*Armageddon* by Artificial Games) and a real-time strategy game based on the bestselling Left Behind series of books (*Left Behind: Eternal Forces* by Left Behind Games). Both games promise to be not only Bible-based, but also realistic and technologically on par with mainstream games developed by companies like THQ and EA Games.

According to Garland Wong, president of Artificial Games, *Armageddon* will be based on popular Christian interpretations of passages in the book of Revelation in the Bible. The story will center around the belief that at some point in the future a "world leader" (that is to say, the Antichrist) will emerge and persecute all those who will not follow him. The game, which may receive an M-rating for its realistic violence and combat, will run "on the state-of-the-art Reality engine" and feature "customizable vehicles, near-future weaponry—and even bloodshed" on a single and multiplayer platform.[3]

Troy Lyndon, CEO of Left Behind Games, makes comparisons between some popular secular titles and the games that will be based on the Tim LaHaye and Jerry Jenkins novels:

> Gamers who like *StarCraft, Warcraft III, Command & Conquer,* and *Rise of Nations,* as well as more recent RTS releases, will love our game.…Many of the hidden clues you'll find will make for some off-the-chart amazing coffee-table discussion material. We believe gamers are intelligent; our game has more intellectual content and concepts than seen in a typical game. It's not a bunch of hoo-ha for the sake of calling it a Christian game.[4]

Other Christian video games slated to hit the market soon show that many in the religious community are welcoming the draw and influence of the world's newest entertainment form. And if the multimillion-dollar Christian retail sales market for religious music, books, and novelty products is any indication of what awaits Christian video games, then the Christian video-game industry will be here to stay.

Parting Shots

When I attended the *World of Warcraft (WoW)* convention in October 2005, I was able to meet many different players of *WoW* for the first time. They came from numerous countries: Bulgaria, France, Germany, Canada, to name but a few. And all of them, like me, had come to have a good time and meet people they had spoken to only online during game play. It was an exciting event that allowed new friendships to be forged and old online friendships to be solidified. This is one of the main aspects of video games that continues to draw players: fellowship, companionship, and friendship.

As one 20-year-old told me, the reason he plays video games for several hours a day is for the "teamwork and sense of personal accomplishment" he derives from the game, especially when it comes to the "challenge of problem solving" that goes along with finishing quests. Another 20-something who flew to California from Canada revealed her reasons for playing *WoW*, saying, "It's the friendship with others and meeting new people."

Before entering the 2005 *World of Warcraft* convention, thousands of fans and players had to wait for hours in a line that wrapped around the huge Anaheim, California, Convention Center. I met attendees from all over the United States (Maryland, Kansas, Florida, Michigan) and the world (Australia, Canada, Belgium, Germany).

The number-one reason people gave me for traveling so far was "to meet friends" that had been made while playing the game online. Video-gaming is a highly social pastime that must be recognized as a major source of friendship and camaraderie for a whole new generation. (Photos by Richard Abanes.)

Interestingly, many of the young players I spoke to during the convention also mentioned that a significant number of kids and teens want very much to include their parents in their gaming activities—if only their parents were willing to play with them. A 23-year-old remarked, "Even if the parents aren't very good, it doesn't matter. It would just be great to have them there. It would mean a lot to kids."

In other words, rather than fearing video games, parents, educators, and church leaders should embrace them as a new way of connecting with the younger generation. They can be fun, instructional, and therapeutic (intellectually, emotionally, physically, *and* spiritually), not to mention helpful in the creation of deep friendships and family relationships.

To benefit from video games simply requires some caution and knowledge about what is out there. It is my hope that the previous pages will help you—the reader and the player—find the best of video games for yourself, friends, and family.

As for me, I am off to spend a few hours playing *Eve Online*—my favorite game of all. It is time—*finally* time—for me to buy and fly a brand-new battle cruiser called a Ferox. I have been training for it since the start of my work on this book. Now, several months later, the piloting skills I need have been obtained, and I have enough Interstellar Kredits (space money) to make my purchase…so I can zoom off into the cosmos. Look out, space pirates—*here I come!*

Notes

The Next Generation

Epigraph. Brady Fiechter, "The Art of the Game," *Play*, Oct. 2005, p. 28.

1. Patrick Klepek, "Frag to the Music," *Computer Gaming World*, Apr. 2005, p. 33.

2. Benjamin Porcari, quoted in "Rock Stars in Excess," interview, *Play*, Oct. 2005, p. 115.

3. David Jenkins, "Video Games to Lead Entertainment Growth," Oct. 6, 2005, www.gamasutra.com; "Direct to Videogames," *PlayStation 2 Magazine*, July 2005, p. 8; "Newsbytes: The Men Who Loved Games," *Computer Games*, July 2005, p. 34.

4. Information available at www.gameriot.com.

5. "Newsbytes," *Computer Games*, Nov. 2005, p. 56.

6. Colin Campbell, "IBC Digital," *Next Generation*, Oct. 3, 2005, www.next-gen. biz.

7. Advertisement flyer, "Video Games North American Tour: 2005 Live"; Roger Altizer, "Dear Friends: Music from Final Fantasy Tours North America," http://playstation.about.com.

8. "Charles Hirschhorn: Founder/CEO G4 Television," interview, *Game Informer* #146, p. 34; "Tap Across America," *Play*, Oct. 2005, p. 14.

9. Klepek, p. 33.

10. "Newsbytes—Salvation," *Computer Games*, www.cgonline.com, p. 33; Garland Wong, quoted in "Games with a Calling," *GamePro*, Nov. 2005, pp. 73, 80.

11. Troy Lyndon, quoted in "Games with a Calling," pp. 73-80.

12. Henry Jenkins and Kurt Squire, "This Polygon for Sale," *Computer Games*, Sept. 2005, www.cgonline.com, p. 94.

13. Benjamin Spock, quoted in Steve Bauman, "For Mature Industries Only," *Computer Games*, July 2005, www.cgonline.com, p. 13.

14. "Won't Someone Think of the Childen?" *PC Gamer* (UK edition), Oct. 2005, p. 12.

15. Leland Yee, interview, *PC Gamer,* Dec. 2005, p. 38.

16. Jay Reeves, "Moore Gets Death for Killing Three at Rural Alabama Police Office," *Everything Alabama,* Oct. 6, 2005.

17. John Davison, "Pop Culture Pariah," *Computer Gaming World*, p. 17.

18. Davison, p. 17.

19. Elias G., letter to editor, *Play,* Oct. 2005, p. 10.

20. "Thread: Gaming Photography," message board thread, reprinted in *PC Gamer,* Oct. 2005, p. 51.

21. Rory Armes, quoted in "Show Us Some Emotion," *Electronic Gaming Monthly*, April 2005, p. 70.

22. "Kick Ass," *PC Gamer* (UK edition), Sept. 2005, p. 124.

23. "Sony Owns Your Brain," *Game Informer* #146, p. 31.

Chapter 1: Coming to Terms—From RPG to FPS

Epigraph. Jamil Moledina, "Getting Our Unique Story Straight," *Game Informer* #146, p. 42.

1. Seth Shiesel, quoted in John Davison, "Pop Culture Pariah," *Computer Gaming World*, pp. 17-18.

2. Ryan Scott, " The Elder Scrolls IV: Oblivion," *Computer Gaming World*, Nov. 2005, p. 35.

3. Tom Chick, "The Decline and Fall of the Roman Empire," *Computer Games*, Nov. 2005, pp. 61-63.

4. "The Wright Stuff," *Computer Games*, June 2005, p. 42.

5. Boba Fatt, "Black & White 2," *GamePro*, Nov. 2005, p. 122.

6. Mike Griffin, "Black & White 2," *Play*, Oct. 2005, p. 82.

Chapter 2: The Ratings Game

Epigraph. Quoted in "Quotables," *Computer Games*, Nov. 2005, p. 56.

1. Jamil Moledina, "Getting Our Unique Story Straight," *Game Informer* #146, p. 42.

2. "Direct to Videogames," *PlayStation 2 Magazine*, July 2005, p. 8.

3. "Video Game Sales Reach Record $7.3 Billion," *GameShout News*, www .gameshout.com.

4. Vince Horiuchi, "The Line Between Video Games and Film Is Beginning to Blur," *Salt Lake Tribune*, January 24, 2005, www.sltrib.com.

5. Entertainment Software Rating Board, "Game Rating & Descriptor Guide," www .esrb.org.

6. "ESRB Game Ratings," www.esrb.org.

7. "ESRB Game Ratings," www.esrb.org.

8. "Sex & Violence 2005," *Computer Games*, Sept. 2005, p. 9.

9. Alex Berenson, "Watch Your Back, Harry Potter: A Wizardly Computer Game: Diablo 11 Is a Hot Seller," *New York Times*, Aug. 3, 2000, www.nytimes.com.

10. David Simon, "Bill Saves Kids from Graphic Video Games," *Seattle Post-Intelligencer*, Feb. 27, 2003, http://seattlepi.nwsource.com.

11. Simon, http://seattlepi.newsource.com.

12. Donald E. Cook, *Testimony of the American Academy of Pediatrics on Media Violence Before the U.S. Senate Commerce Committee*, presented Sept. 13, 2000, p. 5; AP, "Parents Search for Family-Friendly Videos Amid a Sea of Mature Games," *Citizen-Times*, Jan. 14, 2005, http://orig.citizen-times.com/cache/article/family/73748.shtml.

13. Susan B. Shor, "Violent Video Games Too Accessible to Kids, Say Watchdogs," *Tech News World*, Nov. 24, 2004, www.technewsworld.com.

14. According to both the 2004 list released by the Interfaith Center on Corporate Responsibility and the 2004 list of the aforementioned Institute on Media and the Family, the most violent and sexually offensive games include several top sellers: *Doom 3; Grand Theft Auto: San Andreas; Half-Line 2;* and *Mortal Combat: Deception*. Other games condemned for their intense violence were *Postal 2, Manhunt,* and *Resident Evil* (see Shor, www.technewsworld.com).

15. A worker from store #1731, as quoted in Maureen Stivers, "Retailer Strikes Back," *Official Playstation Magazine*, Mar. 2005, p. 18.

16. "Resident Evil Evicted," editor's response, *Game Pro*, Nov. 2005, p. 16.

17. John Scalzi, "Too Tired for the First Amendment," *Official Playstation Magazine*, Mar. 2005, p. 66.

18. Peter Cohen, "Industry Groups to Fight California Video Game Law," *Macworld News*, Oct. 11, 2005, www.macworld.com; Lisa Baertlein, "Industry Plans to Sue to Stop Calif. Video Game Law," Oct. 11, 2005, www.extremetech.com.

19. Hal Halprin, interview, *PC Gamer*, Dec. 2005, p. 38.

20. Leland Yee, quoted in Steve Bauman, "Java Blues," *Computer Games*, Oct. 2005, p. 44.

21. Bauman, p. 44.

22. Jack Thompson, quoted in Brett Todd, "Just Like Jack Thompson's Blues," *Computer Games*, Oct. 2005, p. 86.

23. Spencer28, letter to editor, *PC Gamer*, Nov. 2005, p. 8.

24. Jack Thomson, press conference, quoted in *Computer Games*, June 2005, p. 43.

25. John Davison, "Pop Culture Pariah," *Computer Gaming World,* Oct. 2005, p. 18.

Chapter 3: Mature Means Mature, Part One

Epigraph. "Charles Hirschhorn: Founder/CEO G4 Television," interview, *Game Informer*, #146, p. 34.

1. "Scalding Hot Coffee," *PC Gamer* (UK edition), Oct. 2005, p. 16.

2. Doug Lowenstein, interview, "Trust the System," *Computer Games*, Oct. 2005, pp. 46-47.

3. Jack Thompson, quoted in Steve Bauman, "Java Blues," *Computer Games,* Oct. 2005, p. 46; Bauman, p. 47.

4. See quoted speech in John Davison, "Pop Culture Pariah," *Computer Gaming World*, Oct. 2005, p. 19.

5. Thompson, quoted in Bauman, pp. 44-45; Jack Thompson, quoted in Brett Todd, "Just Like Jack Thompson's Blues," *Computer Games,* Oct. 2005, p. 86.

6. "Scalding Hot Coffee," p. 16.

7. Author's summary and paraphrase of various letters sent to gaming magazines such as *PC Gamer, Computer Gaming World,* and *Game Informer.*

8. "Sex &Violence 2005," *Computer Games,* Sept. 2005, p. 9.

9. "Sex &Violence 2005," p. 9.

10. See Media Awareness Network, "How Marketers," www.media-awareness.ca.

11. Jean-Christophe Guyot, "Prince of Persia 2—Official Movie 2," http://games. channel.aol.com.

12. Guyot, available at http://games.channel.aol.com/videos.adp?gameID=14586.

13. Levi Buchanan, video clips available at www.gamespot.com; cf. "Crime and Punishment: 'Punisher' Takes a Different Approach to Its Violence," *Chicago Tribune,* Jan. 27, 2005, www.chicagotrib.com.

14. I played this game for several hours on numerous days in January 2005.

15. "Bill Summary & Status for the 107th Congress," http://thomas.loc.gov/cgi-bin/bdquery/z?d107:s.0792:. This bill would be known as the "Media Marketing Accountability Act."

16. "Joe Lieberman," *Wikipedia: The Free Encyclopedia,* http://en.wikipedia.org/wiki/ Joseph_Lieberman#Video_game_censorship.

17. Eric Harris, videotaped dialogue with Dylan Klebold, homemade video. Harris also made references to *Doom* on his Web site, which included an "illustration of a man shooting automatic pistols, a large monster with horns, and a boy, eyes wide, pointing two pistols. In big red letters, it says: 'I hate you. Eric Harris owns every

single one of you....*Doom* will become reality!'" (Jodi Wilgoren and Dirk John-son, "Sketch of 2 Killers: Contradictions and Confusion," *New York Times*, Apr. 23, 1999, www.nytimes.com). In his America Online profile, Harris also noted under his hobbies, "Professional doom and doom 2, creator."

18. See video clips and advertisements at www.gamespot.com.

19. Andrew Park, "F.E.A.R.: First Encounter Assault and Recon," *GameSpot*, Jan. 18, 2005, www.gamespot.com.

20. Park, www.gamespot.com.

21. Greg Kasavin (executive director of *GameSpot*), "Greg Kasavin Reviews the Violent Action Game from Rockstar Games," *GameSpot*, Apr. 20, 2004, www.gamespot. com.

22. Daphne White, "The 'Dirty Little Secret' About Video Games," *The Lion & Lamb Project Newsletter*, Summer/Fall 1999, www.lionlamb.org/news_2_2_1.html.

23. "Duke Nukem," advertisement, http://maxpages.com.

Chapter 4: Mature Means Mature, Part Two

Epigraph: Fernando Garcia, "Taking Women in Games Seriously," letter to editor, *GamePro*, Nov. 2005, p. 14.

1. National Organization for Women, "NOW–NYC Fact Sheet on Violent Video Games," www.nownyc.org/video_factsheet.htm.

2. Helen Grieco, "Statement from California National Organization for Women (NOW) Executive Director," Dec. 2003, www.canow.org/news/press/video%20game%20statement.doc.

3. Jhanidya Bermeo, letter to editor, *GamePro*, Nov. 2005, p. 18.

4. Garcia, "Taking Women in Games Seriously," p. 14.

5. "Taking Women in Games Seriously," editor's response, *GamePro*, Nov. 2005, p. 14.

6. Tom Loftus, "Game Mocks Real Tragedy, Gang Experts Say," Nov. 6, 2004, http://msnbc.msn.com/id/6409148/.

7. Loftus, http://msnb.msn.com/id/6409148/; José Perez, quoted in Loftus, http://msnbc.msn.com/id/6409148/.

8. Stephen Cliff, quoted in Loftus, http://msnb.msn.com/id/6409148/; Lisa Taylor-Austin, quoted in Loftus, http://msnbc.msn.com/id/6409148/.

9. "Capcom/Nuby Tech Team Up for RE4 Chainsaw Controller," Nov. 17, 2004, www.gameinformer.com.

10. Nuby Tech, "Nuby Tech Reveals Horrifying Resident Evil 4 Chainsaw Controller for Nintendo GameCube," Nov. 16, 2004, www.nubytech.com.

11. Donald E. Cook, *Testimony of the American Academy of Pediatrics on Media Violence Before the U.S. Senate Commerce Committee,* presented Sept. 13, 2000, p. 5; AP, "Parents Search for Family-Friendly Videos Amid a Sea of Mature Games," *Citizen-Times,* Jan. 14, 2005, http://orig.citizen-times.com/cache/article/family/73748.shtml.

12. "America's Army," *King Mongo Pro Game Reviewer,* www.noapologiespress.com/editorial/mongo/americasarmy.html.

13. Gary Webb, "The Killing Game," Oct. 14, 2004, *Sacramento News & Review,* www.newsreview.com/issues/sacto/2004-10-14/cover.asp.

14. Michael Peck, "Air Force's Latest Video Game Targets Potential Recruits," Jan. 2005, *National Defense Magazine,* www.nationaldefensemagazine.org/issues/2005/Jan/AirForceLatestVideoGame.htm.

15. Michael Peck, "'America's Army' Fan Base Expanding," Dec. 2004, *National Defense Magazine,* www.nationaldefensemagazine.org/issues/2004/Dec/AmericasArmy Fan.htm.

16. Webb, www.newsreview.com/issues/sacto/2004-10-14/cover.asp.

17. U.S. Army, "America's Army: Support—FAQ," www.americasarmy.com/support/faq_win.php.

18. U.S. Army, "America's Army: Support—FAQ," www.americasarmy.com/support/faq_win.php.

19. Webb, www.newsreview.com/issues/sacto/2004-10-14/cover.asp.

20. Advertisement, "Close Combat: First to Fight," *MacHome,* Feb. 2005, p. 5.

21. Webb, www.newsreview.com/issues/sacto/2004-10-14/cover.asp.

22. Peck, "'America's Army' Fan," www.nationaldefensemagazine.org/issues/2004/Dec/AmericasArmyFan.htm; cf. Michael Peck, "Successful War Games Combine Both Civilian and Military Traits," Nov. 2003, *National Defense Magazine,* www.nationaldefensemagazine.org/issues/2003/Nov/SuccessfulWar.htm.

23. I watched these advertisements at www.gamespot.com.

24. Nick Turse, "Bringing the War Home: The New Military-Industrial-Entertainment Complex at War and Play," *ZNet Magazine,* Oct. 16, 2003, www.zmag.org/content/showarticle.cfm?ItemID=4361.

25. Turse, www.zmag.org/content/showarticle.cfm?ItemID=4361.

26. Harold Kennedy, "Computer Games Liven Up Military Recruiting, Training," Nov. 2002, *National Defense Magazine,* www.nationaldefensemagazine.org/issues/2002/Nov/Computer_Games.htm.

27. U.S. Army Corp of Engineers, "Commercial Terrain Visualization Software Product Information—Product Name: Full Spectrum Warrior," Sept. 23, 2004, www.tec.army.mil/research/products/TD/tvd/survey/Full_Spectrum_Warrior.html.

28. Bill Gertz, "CIA Pursues Video Game," *Washington Times*, Sept. 29, 2003.

29. Joe Pappalardo, "Demand for Non-Combat Skills Fuels Interest in Games," *National Defense Magazine*, Dec. 2004, www.nationaldefensemagazine.org/issues/2004/Dec/DemandForNonCombatSkills.htm.

30. Peck, "Air Force's Latest Video," www.nationaldefensemagazine.org/issues/2005/Jan/AirForceLatestVideoGame.htm.

31. Billy Cain, quoted in Peck, "Air Force's Latest Video," www.nationaldefensemagazine.org/issues/2005/Jan/AirForceLatestVideoGame.htm. Cain is the vice president of Critical Mass Interactive.

32. As of Jan. 2005, a search on the word "games" at www.nationaldefensemagazine.org retrieved 153 articles. A narrowed search for "video game" received 25 hits and a search for "First-Person Shooter" pulled up 5 hits.

33. Kennedy, www.nationaldefensemagazine.org/issues/2002/Nov/Computer_Games.htm.

34. Alexandre Perni, letter to *Electronic Gaming Monthly*, Sept. 2005, p. 14.

35. Michael Peck, "Army Licenses Game to Entertainment Company," Dec. 2004, *National Defense Magazine*, www.nationaldefensemagazine.org/issues/2004/Dec/ArmyLicenses.htG.

Chapter 5: To Play or Not to Play?

Epigraph. Jennifer Tsao, "Editorial," *Electronic Gaming Monthly*, Oct. 2005, p. 9.

1. Brady Fiechter, "Doom: The Movie," *Play,* Oct. 2005, p. 112.

2. Vince Zampella, quoted in Fiechter, "Call of Duty 2," *Play,* Oct. 2005, p. 44.

3. Duke Ferris, "The Kids Aren't Killing," *PC Gamer*, Nov. 2005, p. 46; Virgin Megastore Top Ten List, *Play*, Oct. 2005, p. 16.

4. Qaaron, letter to editor, *PC Gamer*, Nov. 2005, p. 9.

5. Jennifer Tsao, "No Nookie Allowed," *Electronic Gaming Monthly*, October 2005, p. 68.

6. Steve Johnson, "CGW Interview: Steven Johnson," *Computer Gaming World* #255, p. 20.

7. John Davison, "Pop Culture Pariah," *Computer Gaming World,* Oct. 2005, p. 17.

8. Duke Ferris, "The Kids Aren't Killing," *PC Gamer,* Nov. 2005, p. 44.

9. Ferris, p. 46.

10. David Enna, letter to editor, *Computer Gaming World,* Nov. 2005, p. 26.

11. The Watcher, "Need for Speed: Most Wanted," *GamePro,* Nov. 2005, p. 93.

12. Tsao, "No Nookie," p. 68.

13. www.direct2drive.com.

14. "Can the Cussing," *PC Magazine,* Dec. 2005, p. 13.

15. David Fong, "Getting Good at New Games," *PC Gamer* (UK edition), Oct. 2005, p. 117.

16. Jill Duffy, "Game Developer's Fourth Annual Salary Survey," *Game Career Guide,* Fall 2005, pp. 30-32.

17. "Video Games Play Painkillers," *Techtree News,* www.techtree.com.

18. Dennis McCauley, "The Modern Gamer's Political Manifesto," *Game Informer,* #149, p. 38.

19. Anu Patel, quoted in "Video Games Used to Relax Kids in Hospital," www.abcnews.go.com; "Microsoft Donates Videogames to Childrens Hospital," *FNG Gaming News,* www.fnggaming.com.

20. Mike Snider, "Video Games Actually Can be Good for You," *USA Today,* Sept. 26, 2005, www.usatoday.com.

21. Steve Bauman, "For Mature Industries Only," *Computer Games,* July 2005, p. 13.

22. Ashley Esqueda, "True Crime: New York City," *Play,* Oct. 2005, p. 38.

23. Video Game Sales Reach Record $7.3 Billion," *GameShout News,* Jan 2005, www.gameshout.com/news/012005/article354.htm.

24. Alex Berenson, "Watch Your Back, Harry Potter: A Wizardly Computer Game, Diablo II Is a Hot Seller," *New York Times,* Aug. 3, 2000, www.nytimes.com.

25. Webb, www.newsreview.com/issues/sacto/2004-10-14/cover.asp.

26. The White House, "Talking It Over: Hillary Rodham Clinton," June 2, 2005, http://clinton4.nara.gov/.

27. Donald E. Cook, *Testimony of the American Academy of Pediatrics on Media Violence Before the U.S. Senate Commerce Committee,* presented Sept. 13, 2000, p. 3.

28. Jennifer Tsao, "Editorial," p. 9.

Chapter 6: Family-Friendly Fun

Epigraph. This advertisement appeared in *Play* magazine, Oct. 2005, inside front cover.

1. Chris Morris, quoted in John Davison, "Pop Culture Pariah," *Computer Gaming World,* Oct. 2005, p. 19; Brady Fiechter, "Defining Gameplay," *Play,* Oct. 2005, p. 119.

2. Jim Rossignol, "City of Heroes," *PC Gamer,* Oct. 2005, pp. 125-126.

3. Funky Zealot, "Games with a Calling," *Gamepro,* Nov. 2005, p. 80.

4. Troy Lyndon, quoted in Zealot, p. 80.

Books by Bestselling Author–Journalist Richard Abanes

THE TRUTH BEHIND THE DA VINCI CODE
A Challenging Response to the Bestselling Novel

HARRY POTTER, NARNIA, AND THE LORD OF THE RINGS
What You Need to Know About Fantasy Books and Novels

WHAT EVERY PARENT NEEDS TO KNOW
ABOUT VIDEO GAMES
A Gamer Explores the Good, Bad, and Ugly of the Virtual World

RICK WARREN AND THE PURPOSE THAT DRIVES HIM
An Insider Looks at the Phenomenal Bestseller

BECOMING GODS
A Closer Look at 21st-Century Mormonism

ONE NATION UNDER GODS
A History of the Mormon Church

*For more information about Richard Abanes
and his endeavors, visit*
www.abanes.com/abanesbio.html

What Is Fact? What Is Fiction?
THE TRUTH BEHIND
THE DA VINCI CODE
Richard Abanes

"All descriptions of artwork, architecture, documents, and secret rituals in this novel are accurate."

With those startling words, *The Da Vinci Code*—author Dan Brown's megaselling thriller—kicks you into high gear. After 454 nonstop pages, you've discovered a lot of shocking facts about history and Christianity...or have you?

Award-winning investigative journalist Richard Abanes takes you down to the murky underpinnings of this blockbuster novel and movie that has confused so many people. What do you really learn when the *Code's* assumptions are unearthed and scrutinized?

- **The Code:** Jesus was married to Mary Magdalene, who he named leader of the church before his death.
- **The Truth:** This fantasy has no support even from the "Gnostic gospels" mentioned in the *Code*, let alone from the historical data.
- **The Code:** Since the year 1099, a supersecret society called "The Priory of Sion" has preserved knowledge of Jesus and Mary's descendants.
- **The Truth:** Today's "Priory of Sion" was founded in the early 1960s by a French con man who falsified documents to support the story of Jesus' "bloodline."
- **The Code:** As a "Priory" leader and pagan goddess-worshipper, Leonardo da Vinci coded secret knowledge about Jesus and Mary into his paintings.
- **The Truth:** Da Vinci had no known ties to any secret societies. Any obscure images in his paintings likely reflect his personal creativity.

Probing, factual, and revealing, *The Truth Behind the Da Vinci Code* gives you the straightforward information you need to separate the facts from the fiction.

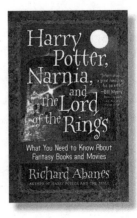

HARRY POTTER, NARNIA, AND THE LORD OF THE RINGS
Richard Abanes

Is every fantasy story appropriate for everyone?

In this evenhanded exploration of the books of J.K. Rowling, C.S. Lewis, and J.R.R. Tolkien, as well as the films based on their writings, Richard Abanes, a fantasy fan himself, answers key questions:

- What is inspiring and healthy in these works? What is misleading and harmful?

- Do I need to be concerned about occult influence from fantasy?

- How do movies and merchandising impact kids' minds?

Pro-literature and pro-fun, *Harry Potter, Narnia, and The Lord of the Rings* helps you evaluate fantasy's strengths and dangers from a balanced Christian perspective.

"Informative...a great resource for parents!"
—BILL MYERS, bestselling youth and children's fiction author